Pearls and Purse Straps... or How a Shrink "Shrinks" Herself

Pearls and Purse Straps... or How a Shrink "Shrinks" Herself

Dr. Beth-Anne Blue

Copyright © 2025 by Dr. Beth-Anne Blue
All rights reserved. No part of this book may be reproduced in any manner whatsoever without written permission except in the case of brief quotations embodied in critical articles and reviews.

Hardcover ISBN:9781950544592
EBook ISBN: 9781950544608

Rand-Smith Publishing

First Printing, 2025

Neither the publisher nor the author is rendering professional advice or services. The information contained herein is not intended as a substitute for consulting with a healthcare professional. Matters regarding health require professional attention and should always be taken seriously.

...to Marjorie & Jason

Warning...

...I felt that I should include a "warning" at the beginning of this book. Some might use the word "triggers." I don't care for that word, so I shall use the word "Warning."

Warning: There are some happy stories, funny stories, and some sad stories in this book. What I can say about that is it is all-inclusive of my life; everything is true to my knowledge, and accurate. Some of the contents contain references to my own mental health for the sake of authenticity, advocacy, admiration, and respect to everyone out there struggling with mental health issues. Stay strong. Stay present.

And, lastly, seek help from the safe people in your life and stay alive. I did. It's been an exhaustive struggle. I am only now living the best life I know how, with the right people in my life. I have lived to see my plays and movies produced, my screenplays win awards and lastly, the publication of this book.

—Beth-Anne Blue

Contents

Dedication **v**
Warning... **vi**
Foreword #1 **xi**
Foreword #2 **xiii**
Foreword #3 **xv**
Acknowledgements **xvi**

1 Why In the World... **1**
2 The Pat-Down... **4**
3 Pearls and Purse Straps... **5**
4 Handstands In the Ocean... **7**
5 Soar... **13**
6 I Wonder... **17**
7 The Love of a Child... **19**
8 A New Box of Crayons... **21**
9 Gifts or Artistry... **23**
10 "Cause I Ain't Got No Color..." **25**
11 A Letter to the Lost... **26**
12 I Don't Have a Choice, Really... **28**

13 The Colors That You Choose to Paint Your Day... 32

14 Sex or Pain... 34

15 "Do You Have an Ending Yet?"... 37

16 Souls On Board... 39

17 Moments... 42

18 Not Now... 44

19 Stand Up Eight... 47

20 Poodle Nightmares and Other Challenges... 49

21 A Perfect Day for Rain... 51

22 College Football & Other Choices... 52

23 My First Suicide... 55

24 Sometimes, a Closed Door is Just a Closed Door... 57

25 Exquisite Pain... 58

26 Gifts and Disabilities... 61

27 The Power of Strangers or Why Therapy Works... 64

28 Prince Charming & Sleeping Beauty, Really... 67

29 Where Does the Sidewalk End... 71

30 Mirrors... 74

31 A Life-Changing Day in Three Parts... 76

32 Safe Versus Unsafe people: A Lesson From Snoopy... 84

33 Poodle Instructions or Paisley's Vocabulary... 87

34 Stella and the Goose... 91

35 The Sign of the Signs... 96

36 I Want Versus I Need... **98**

37 Blessings in Disguise... **101**

38 When to Quit a Job... **104**

39 Be Purposeful... **107**

40 Bollards, Scuppers, and Downspouts, Oh My... **111**

41 Setbacks and Pork Chops... **113**

42 Maximizing Fun Factor... **115**

43 Diversity and Inclusion... **117**

44 The Universe Is Never Wrong... **119**

45 How We Got Paisley... **122**

46 Speaking of Poodles... **127**

47 A Sample... **131**

48 Bob's Barricades... **142**

49 Music... **144**

50 Motherfucking Quality Time... **146**

51 The House, the Kids... **148**

52 The Last Autograph... **150**

53 The "Bystander Effect," NOT... **152**

54 A Final (i.e., Lasting) Word... **155**

55 Sadness, Lobsters, and Existentialism... **157**

56 It Is a Lovely Day... **161**

57 Unnecessary Jostling... **166**

58 A Work In Progress... **169**

About the Author   172

Foreword #1

What's in a name, anyway...?

...so here's the thing. I have a Ph.D. I got it in 1996. Does that qualify me to write a book? I don't think so. If you knew it was a Doctorate in Clinical Psychology, would that make my words more valuable? Maybe.

I have spent almost twenty years practicing psychology. That is correct. Since 1998, I have spent my time in an office face-to-face with people who are requesting my assistance in some sort of mental health capacity. I have been licensed in three states to do this. I have done so in a multitude of environments: private practices, community mental health centers, university counseling centers, Employee Assistance Programs in higher education, etc.

My name loses its aesthetic symmetry when I add the Ph.D. Four letters + four letters + four letters...+ three letters and 2 periods? I don't know. I like my name and how I got it is a bit of a story by itself. You must admit, there is a pleasing symmetry to Beth-Anne Blue. I only started hyphenating my name in graduate school. Legally, my first name is "Beth," and my middle name is "Anne." My mother insisted that I go by "Beth Anne." Easy enough, right? Unfortunately, not.

As an extremely shy and abnormally sensitive child, it was painful to correct every single person who called me Beth.
"I go by Beth-Anne..."
"I go by Beth-Anne..."
"I go by Beth-Anne."

Even the nurse up the street (may she rest in peace) who gave me my allergy shots would send me home crying because she would always call me Beth. My mother had to call her to ask her to call me Beth-Anne. Every day in the second grade, I would come home crying because my teacher would call me Beth.

"Hello, Mrs. Preston, this is Beth-Anne Blue's mother..." My mom called her at least once a week.

As an aside, my aunt's name (mother's sister) is Mary Jane. I think my mom wanted to keep a two-name first name in the family. So, cursed I was. But now I am happy with my name. In fact, I've grown quite fond of it.

To this day, I get all the deviations of Beth-Anne you could imagine...Beth, Mary Anne, Mary Beth, etc. Even hyphenated, people seem to have trouble with a two-name first name. When I got to graduate school and became more assertive, I either had to correct people over and over or just go by Dr. Blue. In the end, I think it worked out for the best. Dr. Blue is easy to remember for my clients. To whatever degree degrees mean, I will be Dr. Beth-Anne Blue for the purpose of this book, meant to help me, *Beth-Anne*.

There is one last way this has been a helpful distinction. When I am out in public, and I hear someone yell out "Dr. Blue," my family knows to keep walking, as it is more than likely a client, someone whose confidence I must ethically maintain. If I am out and someone yells my correct first name, "Beth-Anne," then that means I know them personally, and my family can hang back, as it is likely a friend or colleague.

I realize for the purposes of this book; however, it is best to include my credentials. It is not that it is inauthentic if I do not use my credentials, because I am authentic no matter if I use them or not – but I do want this book to be a combination of my expertise and my own life experience. So, use them, I will.

It is about me, after all: a human being, a psychologist. A little bit of my profession might slip into what you are about to read. I do not tire of being Dr. Blue. It is time for me to wholly and completely integrate and own who Dr. Beth-Anne Blue is...was...and has become. At the end of the day, I mean, really? What's in a name? Jesus, a lot more than I thought! Enjoy yours. Own it. Hyphenate it. Change it. Be it. Embrace it even if it's not as easy as you'd like it to be. It sets you apart. That's what's in a name.

Foreword #2

One-Liner(s)...

...I hate to say it...there are going to be two more forewords to this book. Let me get to them. You might want to know to whom this book is dedicated. They are my biological parents, Marjorie and Jason. While married, their forces collided and spit out me and my brother.

They divorced when I was about ten years old. This divorce shaped who I am, for better or for worse. This book is about my journey, and as I look back now, my journey would be quite different if not for the divorce.

My mom was there with me throughout. I owe a lot to her. A long time ago, when we both believed I was special enough to be famous, she always staked her claim in that by saying, "I get to share your first limousine ride!" Even when I told her about my agent agreeing to take on this book for representation, literally, the first thing she said was, "Remember, I get the first limo ride," as if I had forgotten. It was at that time I told her the book was dedicated to her. I am still not sure that is enough for her to feel included in my accomplishments.

Don't get me wrong, our relationship hasn't always been easy. Like any mother-daughter relationship, it's had its ups and downs. Good times and bad. Spoken and unspoken. Whenever I would tell her I had started a new writing project, she would consistently ask two questions: 1) "Does it have an ending yet?" And 2) "Just give me the 'one-liner.'" In other words, what's the bottom line, as if she didn't have time for the story, the journey, the process; she just wanted the point.

In deference to her, I have included a "One-Liner" at the end of each chapter. I've learned a new word, in publishing jargon, that this is considered a "prescriptive" book. There is a moral to each story; or a lesson, if you will. As homage to my mother's shorthand, there is a "One-Liner(s)" summarizing the moral of each story. Some are just one sentence, some are longer.

They are what the story means to me; and what I would like them to mean to you. Take them, leave them, but please read them. Considering using them in your life as applicable. Remember them, live by them. In this world of wellness and trying to get my clients to understand that therapy is a process, these "tools" are meant to be incorporated into your life, as they have been mine, as bottom-line, prescriptive mores to help you live the well-deserved, meaningful life you were meant to live.

Be well.

Foreword #3

Ellipses...

...some might ask, as you read, why all the ellipses? Why all the three dots in the title, in every chapter, and throughout the book? That is because my life is a work in progress. It is my way of saying that I am summarizing, giving you the important elements without providing every little detail and nuance. Technically, an ellipsis means an omission of sorts, of words, or of thoughts. In my case, I use it as if to say, "There might be more to this... but this is what I know." In other words, don't stop reading, as there may be much more to it than what I am writing. I did think of naming the book *Ellipses*, but that didn't really have quite the ring I had hoped. However, it does mean: ...stay tuned... stay present... pay attention... and please keep reading.

Acknowledgements

...I would like to thank, by first name only, Marjorie, Jason (in peace), Phil, David, Douglas, Danielle, Bella, Violet, Ron, Jan, and Paisley. Each of you, I hope, knows the contribution you've made to my life.

To (my other) Douglas, Carole and Tony (in peace), Jordan, Teddy and Margot: you are always on my mind.

I would like to include Marcia, Jackie, Roberta (in peace), Dr. Michael and Diane, for staying with me over the years.

Lastly, I want to thank the higher education system, for without them keeping me educated and employed all these years, there may be no stories to tell.

{ 1 }

Why In the World...

Would a Shrink "Shrink" Herself...?

...other than the catchy alliteration, for me, there seem to be a few reasons. I have been in therapy a few times in my life. Has it worked? Maybe. Everyone's measures of successful therapy are different. What I can tell you about my experience is that having helped others for twenty years has, surprisingly, helped me the most. Every time I see a client, every time I have a session, every time I witness a breakthrough with a client, I am helped in some way. I have my own form of breakthrough. I learn from every client, from every session, from every issue presented to me for help, I have grown. I pay attention; I am present for every moment of every hour that I spend with someone.

Therein lies what I believe is going on. When asked, I tell my clients that this is my gift to them as a mental health professional: that I am one hundred percent present for every minute of our time together. And because I listen closely, I watch closely, and I am fully present, I am somehow helping myself as well. It must sound strange, but I will tell you that I have always said that the minute I stop learning from my clients is the moment I need to get out of the business.

I am still learning, so I'm still practicing. I can also tell you that this is the way I leave "work at work" and don't take it home with me. Because I am present, aware, and experiencing the same things my clients are, I can easily leave things behind at work. I know I gave everything during our time together. And because I have done that, I often cannot answer the following questions from my husband when I get home: "How was your day today? What sorts of clients did you see?" I honestly do not remember. I gave it my all, and I left it there.

As I tell my clients quite simply: Pay attention, be present, listen, and learn not just in our sessions but in your life. If you don't, you may likely end up on my couch wondering what you missed out on. I am certainly not saying that I catch it all with my clients or myself. What I am saying is maybe get off the couch or stay on it, but never stop paying attention, never stop being authentic, never stop being present, and never stop learning. One can do that on or off the couch (meaning in or out of therapy). I'll give you my time and attention, if you will allow yourself to pay attention and be present in your own life.

I don't think life is about either being happy or being sad. I think it is about being present and aware as much of the time as possible so as not to miss the moments of happiness or contentedness that come your way or the moments of sadness that befall you. Because if you are going to be present, you must commit to being present in the good and in the bad. The rest of it is usually things that will pass, or maybe they won't. But if you are present and paying attention all the time, you are sure not to miss the good stuff and "make your way" through the bad stuff. So, here is a collection of my moments. I am grateful for every story you are about to read, for writing is my way of doing therapy with myself.

Enjoy.

PEARLS AND PURSE STRAPS... OR HOW A SHRINK "SHRINKS" HERSELF ~ {3}

One-Liner: This is a once-in-a-lifetime chance to read exactly how a psychologist would conduct therapy with herself. After twenty-plus years of practice, this is how I've made it through my life: writing. I hope you'll come along for this opportunity to go inside the mind of a psychologist and read how I would "treat" myself. Slowly work on being present in your own life by reminding yourself to become fully engaged in your every experience.

{ 2 }

The Pat-Down...

...so, I recently got a full pat-down by the TSA at the airport. As I stood there, my arms stretched out, feet shoulder-width, essentially being fondled by a female agent, I realized I had a choice. I could be embarrassed and a bit humiliated, thinking of everyone looking at me, wondering why I was holding up the line. Or I could choose to shift my focus away from my surroundings; instead, focus on what was happening to me and how I was handling it.

I listened to the agent's voice: *Would you like a private pat-down?... Pull your jeans up... Untuck your shirt... Raise your arms above your head.* I did exactly what she told me to do. She even swabbed my hands. I waited patiently again, choosing not to be self-conscious, anxious, or embarrassed about the line I was creating. I chose to stay in the moment. In my moment. *Fuck! Don't worry about everybody else.* They were going to have to wait one way or another since it was the holiday season...in an airport. C'mon, people...if *I* was the worst thing that happened to them that day, they had bigger problems.

One-Liner: I'll say it again...if I was the worst thing that happened to people in that security line that day, then that was their issue, not mine. Don't stress over the little things: 1) because they're all minor in the grand scheme of life; and 2) if you do, you'll miss the things that really matter, especially during the holidays.

{ 3 }

Pearls and Purse Straps…

...everyone who knows me will tell you that two things matter in my exterior or external life, meaning the self I present to the world…or maybe just one thing: my accessories. Specifically, my jewelry and my handbags. Once through security after my pat-down on that same trip, I realized I did not have my beloved (okay, that might be an exaggeration, "beloved") pearl necklaces that I wear almost everywhere. They were not on my body or in my personal belongings. I only hoped I had remembered to pack them.

As soon as I was safely through security and not deemed a "flight risk," I found my seat on the airplane. That's when I realized that the strap on my vintage Gucci carry-on bag had broken—snapped clean off. Shit! That's the problem with buying vintage; things might be a bit more fragile than new merchandise.

At that moment, despite passengers still maneuvering to their seats, I took the time to lean into full awareness (mind you, this was pre-COVID) that I was without my pearls and a functioning carry-on bag, vintage or not. Irritated by accepting that this was to be my lot on this particular adventure of travel, I decided to make the best of it and settled in for the flight. I reached into my now broken carry-on for some reading material.

This included, on this particular adventure of travel, a play I had been writing and some educational, work-related material. Pleasure or business? Almost to continue punishing myself, I chose the "business" reading. It was an article I had been meaning to read on the Spanish term, *una personal educada*. It might be worth pointing out that I like to think of myself as fluent in Spanish. I am not. Nonetheless, I found myself reading the article for personal and professional reasons, as its subject matter was intriguing: individual humility. It was about understanding that our lives are a series of constant reminders of our humility. By this, I mean that a few different life choices, and I would have been a completely different person in different circumstances: with pearls and a functioning vintage, Gucci bag. Alas, I had neither.

Without those things, I was uncomfortable, but no one else cared. Why should they? I care, but just like being patted down by the TSA, now it was my turn. No pearls...and bags with broken straps. If those are the worst things that happen in my day, my life isn't so bad.

One-Liner: Please keep things in perspective...a broken purse is a broken purse; a misplaced pearl necklace, is a misplaced pearl necklace. They are nothing more and nothing less, just exactly what they are. The key is to remember not to misdirect your energy into negativity just because life happens. Things don't always go to plan, but you are on an adventure! Be on the ride.

(As an aside, existential questions are asked across all cultures. I will return to some of them later.)

{ 4 }

Handstands In the Ocean...

...was the original title of this book. As it evolved, however, it became clear that the current title embodied more of the content than "handstands in the ocean" (though I may still use that title for something else someday). Nonetheless, this story was what began the process of creating this book.

I was having lunch with my friend, Roberta, a few years ago. She was a coworker. For all intents and purposes, she is the single most reason I accepted my job at the University of Florida (in 2002). I met her at one of my interviews. We hit it off instantly and were friends ever since.

One day, prior to our lunch, I was trying to explain to Roberta, in what I now see as the most selfish way possible, that I wasn't getting enough from our friendship. This behavior is typical for me. I tend to make friends with people who are outgoing and gregariously friendly. The only problem is that most people are attracted to people like that, making intimate friendships with them quite difficult. In any case, Roberta made plans to have lunch with me later that week.

Just because we feel something doesn't make it true, and from all who knew her, Roberta neither neglected her friendships nor avoided the responsibility of friendships...she gave as much as she had to her friendships...I can see that now. I hope this makes sense; feelings are not facts. My feeling that she cared less about me than her other friendships was not actually what was happening. I was being an overly sensitive and needy friend. Just because we feel something doesn't actually make it true. I think it will serve us well to remember that as we all navigate this world of friendships.

Again, before the lunch, for Christmas, Roberta had given me a ceramic plaque with an angel on it. Its inscription read, "You are a gift." Despite never having seen me as that, the sentiment was beautiful. I loved Roberta with all of my heart. That was my gift to her. However, it was a real challenge for me to see myself, my being, my essence, as a gift to anyone's life.

Back to my story...to have met Roberta is to have loved her. Her eyes radiated with a kind of charisma that drew people to her immediately. Her energy was amazing. Her charm was captivating. If I used the word blessing, I would have certainly considered her that. Me, I just felt lucky to know her and so affected by our friendship, whichever state it was in.

Two more digressions, if you'll allow. When I first arrived in a new town to start my job, I found the adjustment to be difficult and emotional. There were times I would just sit at my desk and cry. I would close the door and have a "moment," as I called them, and I had many throughout the year. My grandmother passed away shortly after I moved, adding to my difficult adjustment. Because Roberta's office was across the hall from mine, it was impossible for her not to notice my "moments." I confided in Roberta that I had struggled with depression over the years and that those closest to me hadn't always responded in helpful ways. I suppose there isn't one correct way to respond to someone who is in emotional pain, but I learned there are certainly unhelpful or less helpful ways.

Despite our friendship waxing and waning over the years, I will never forget some of the comforting words Roberta said to me. Two incidents stand out. The first happened when I was having a "moment" in her office. She looked at me and asked what I had hoped so many before her would ask: "What should I do if I notice that you are sad?" In all my years of friends, coworkers, family, boyfriends, bosses, and colleagues, not a single one of them had asked me that question. Maybe they didn't know how to ask it. Maybe there, they were not comfortable and hesitated to get too involved. But Roberta had no such hesitation, and her words sliced through my grief at lightning speed. In a matter of seconds, I was overcome with a profound sense of being heard and understood.

The second incident came much later. Having yet another moment in her office, Roberta looked at me and said, "You are beautiful when you cry." That one statement stopped me in my tracks. I don't think I can explain how that made me feel. All my life, I had heard things like, "Quit your crying" and "No more tears." No one responded to me by trying to understand the reasons behind my tears. Her simple, direct declaration was a sentiment I will never forget.

I recently came across a greeting card with a quote on it from the poet Langston Hughes. I bought it in a pet store, of all places. It reads: *When people care for you, they can straighten out your soul.* I believe in my heart that Roberta was put in my life to help me straighten out my soul.

Getting back to our lunch that day, we had a delightful, albeit brief, visit. We were walking back to our building, and Roberta began telling me a story. "Okay, so I was doing handstands in the ocean the other day..." I stopped walking, struck once again by the beautiful simplicity that was Roberta. Handstands in the ocean? Handstands in the ocean? Who does handstands in the ocean? Roberta did. And I'm sure she was good at it, being the athlete extraordinaire that she was. Me? I was lamenting some back pain and disc problems.

As she continued, her story quickly lost its humorous appeal and took a turn for the worse when she told me about how the same ocean that had allowed her acrobatics had betrayed her. The tidal pull in the water had caused her hands to give away. She collapsed, falling on her head and jamming her neck. She was not seriously injured, but her having fun in the ocean stopped there. I sent Roberta the card about straightening out your soul and wrote, "Here's to doing handstands in the ocean."

Even when we are doing something fun, we still have to be careful. Life has a way of changing direction when we least expect it, which is why we need to love each other and to be loved through the good and the bad times. As long as you can surround yourself with good people, it is then that your soul can get straightened out.

One-Liner: To feel heard, loved, and accepted is to feel unconditional love; never ever turn your back to that, especially since life has a way of dropping you on your head when you are least expecting.

Post-Script: Roberta's life came to a tragic end on March 13, 2018. We had lost touch over the years but did have lunch about a month or two before she passed. She passed from an ascending aortic dissection, which blocked the flow of blood to her brain instantly and completely. This happened as she jumped in a pool at the YMCA before work. Her husband had just completed his laps in the pool. When he last spoke to her, he asked if she was sure she wanted to do it because the water was pretty cold. There are very few heated pools in Florida.

Per her husband, she said to him, "I can do anything you can do," before he left to start his day, and her to start her laps.

She was brain-dead instantly. I understand she was pulled from the water, already unconscious. I don't know the details. I don't really want to know them. She ended up on life support that day at the local teaching hospital. From what I understand, she was "brain-dead," and they removed life support before both of her children could get there. My understanding is that it took several hours for her to pass once they removed the equipment, proving what we already knew of the strength of her character and body.

She was an exquisite human being; she was a beautiful soul. I miss her, even though she was not part of my daily life. Her life was truly cut short. Though she may have been sixty-five years old, she was the kind of person that anyone else was embarrassed to be friends with, not just because of her beauty and charm but because of her extreme dedication to taking care of herself—yoga, bicycling, swimming, etc. She took diligent care of herself...except going to the doctor. If my memory serves, I don't remember her ever going to the doctor. This can be a good thing – or a bad thing depending on how one views self-care. At this point, it doesn't matter. But it took her from us. It was a sad time for the many, no, all of the souls she touched. For those of us who knew her (e.g., her family, her clients, her friends, her colleagues) and from whom she was taken, it was an utterly dark and tragic day for all.

This isn't just me only remembering the good things about her, as we often do when people die. But this I can honestly say from the depths of my soul: It was a truly tragic end to a beautiful life.

One Liner: I believe that all human beings' lives consist of at least two acts, two parts... two stories... or two developmental stages. Unfortunately, we don't all get a second act in life; Roberta certainly didn't get her second act. Sure, we might "plan" for our second acts, i.e., retirement, being closer to family, etc., but it is critical to sprinkle parts of what we have planned for the second act into the first, as we are able. What Roberta's life and death have taught me is that we must always appreciate the beauty of others who are right in front of us TODAY, as tomorrow is promised to no one.

One Liner #2: Just because we feel something is happening doesn't actually make it true. Feelings are not facts. If you aren't sure what is the truth versus what you feel…ASK.

{ 5 }

Soar...

...from 2002-2010, it was part of my job while at the University of Florida to educate its students and community about the dangers of sexual assault (and high-risk drinking, as they often go together), while in college. It was as part of this role that I attended a sexual assault awareness and prevention conference. It was in New Orleans back in March 2003. All the keynote speakers were either survivors of sexual assault, prosecutors, police officers, or those who had chosen to champion the cause of protecting sexual assault victims' rights.

It was an emotional conference for me, listening to all the awful stories and difficult topics. I had done well keeping my own emotions in check until the last day. The speaker was a fairly renowned person in this arena, but I had never heard her speak. She addressed the attendees on the last day of the conference over lunch. As an aside, I usually go to these conferences by myself, purposefully. I generally don't mingle, make contacts or otherwise "network" at things like this. Because in my regular job, I am "on" all the time, I prefer to be anonymous. I have been known to wear jeans, overalls, and the like and just sort of fade in the background. Funny, now I know why I have a Ph.D., so I can wear overalls to a conference and not really give a shit. Huh, suddenly, it all makes sense!

Suffice it to say that I did a fairly good job remaining stoic and professional, even in my overalls, until her talk on the last day. She spoke about survivors of sexual assault. She spoke about surviving her own sexual assault. She spoke about living. She spoke about choosing not to die. From time to time, people in this area talk about sexual assault leaving a victim with a "broken soul." Until this day, however, I had never heard a survivor use the words "broken soul." But I heard it today.

A broken soul. It occurred to me then, at that moment, that I had a broken soul. My soul has been broken for years. Not my heart. Not my brain. But my soul. The inner pain in my soul still consumes me at times. It hasn't for a while; but sometimes I sense that I am clinging to the edge of sanity. Occasionally, I peer over the edge into the abyss of insanity, and that was one of those days.

I held it together for the most part while she was speaking. Then, she decided to show a video. As part of her own recovery, she skydives on the anniversary of the assault. The notion caught on, and now several hundred women jump out of planes all over the country with her once a year. In some circles, this is a well-known event. As part of her talk, she showed a video of her very first jump. It was a tandem, which was particularly difficult for her since she had been attacked from behind. She set the video to Sheryl Crow's song "Soak Up the Sun." Watching the video shoved me over the edge. I had done so well at the conference, but suddenly...watching that video...I could no longer pretend to be personally unaffected by sexual assault.

The video was shown on a movie theatre-size screen. The song was loud, the images quite visceral. Tears began rolling down my cheeks as I watched her flying through the air...soaring... Flying free. Being free. Being unburdened. Letting go of what had happened to her. I watched her soar through space, only to be reminded of my recurrent dream that I could fly.

It happens all the time in my dreams. I fly in them. Some say that is indicative of wanting to be set free of something that may be holding you back. Flying allows you to become unrestrained by whatever keeps you tethered. Sitting there was overwhelming. I wanted to let go, too. I wanted to soar. Jumping out of an airplane, though? Do I really need to do that to feel free? At that moment, I would have signed up to jump out of an airplane without even thinking about it. As I look back on it now, I suppose the second closest way to fly and be free is to die. Dying would set me free. Dying would stop the pain. My soul might be fixed, full, and free.

Boy, are there days that that truly seems a viable option. Maybe that's what my tears were for. Not just for her and her own recovery but for mine, which at that moment was overwhelming. I continued to think, trails of tears cascading down my face. By the way, no one said a word to me at the conference table.

Maybe that's why I now run a sexual assault outreach program. Some believe there are no accidents. I don't have a logical explanation for why I took the job running the sexual assault clinic at the University of Florida other than it got me out of my former job, which was in private practice. I needed a change, but it took a while for me to come to that realization.

So, there I was, fighting the good fight. I don't know why. On most days, it is okay. I don't cry on most days. My soul feels empty most days, but I'm used to that. Maybe I didn't choose this job. Maybe it chose me. I'd say it is part of my healing, but I'm not sure. I know I feel empty at times. I know my soul feels broken. So far, I have chosen to live. I have certainly fallen off the "cliff" many times. But even falling into the dark abyss of the cliff allows me to soar, albeit briefly, and each time I do soar, in my dreams or in front of a big screen, my heart gets a little lighter, my soul a little less burdened.

One-Liner: Soar...whatever that means to you. Stay among the living...just don't let anything ever hold you back from being the best version of yourself, and if something tries to hold you down, soar anyway...

{ 6 }

I Wonder...

...about my friend who died of cervical cancer a few years ago. She was a childhood friend who I had lost touch with until she became sick. Her family had immigrated from Sweden to the United States; I was ten or eleven when we met. As neighbors, we became fast friends. My mom put me in charge of acculturating her. We went our separate ways in junior high and high school and then completely lost touch after graduation.

Her death had been swift, the cancer indiscriminate. Despite the fact that we had lost touch, her family asked me to speak at her funeral. These days I think of her often. She was thirty-three when she died. I know from years of experience that most parents never truly heal after the death of a child, nor should they. How could they? In comparison to other mammals, humans have relatively fewer offspring, investing quite a bit more time, energy, and resources into those we do have, making it that much more devastating to lose one. It is not the natural order of things, having to watch your child die. It's not right; it's not fair; it will never be okay.

In my grief for her, I wrote to her, writing a page in my journal almost daily for a year. My goal was to keep her up to date on my life. I didn't put a time limit on it, but I wrote my last entry exactly one year after her death. Then I was thinking about her one sad morning, and I began to wonder.

I wonder...
I wonder if you hear music in heaven.
I wonder if you hear rain.
I wonder if you smell smells.
I wonder why you are there.
I wonder why I still grieve for you every day.
I wonder why some days are worse than others.
I wonder what inspires you in heaven; or maybe you need not be inspired.
I wonder if you are at peace.
I wonder if you see those who have gone before you.
I wonder if you really are in heaven.
I wonder if I have enough faith to believe you are there.
I wonder if you understand the pain and sadness you left behind.
I wonder if you can give me a sign that you're okay, that your spirit is alive somewhere.
But mostly, I just wonder why you left us and if you really are in a better place.

-b.a.blue

One-Liner: Since we never know when the Universe will take one of our own, your best recourse is to be present every single day you are with your loved ones; and never, ever forget to wonder.

{ 7 }

The Love of a Child...

...sounds easy enough, winning or having the love of a child. Kids love everyone, right? Like dogs or animals, they love attention. While that may be true there is something exceptionally gratifying about receiving love from a child, and especially one that is not your own.

I counseled adults and adolescents for years before I chose to counsel younger children. Initially, they scared me. They were too real for me, too raw, too exposed. I used to say to my colleagues, "I just don't have a good rapport with kids." Or "they just don't like me." I honestly felt like I just couldn't relate to children. Adolescents, I loved counseling them. But anyone under the age of ten scared the shit out of me.

As I matured as a psychologist and as a person, it slowly became clear to me. I didn't have to "have" rapport with a child. I needed to take them as they are or not at all. Use their words. Play their games. Be honest and truthful with them, and most likely, I will get it back. No secrets, no tricks. Just be myself. That's the only rule.

Adults are rule-bound, and they can be repressed, fake, insincere, and self-centered. And a lot of times, they don't always show love for something in return. Many adults fear the raw honesty and vulnerability a child offers in return for love. I did for a long time. When I learned to let go of my own fear and embrace my own vulnerability, that is when I truly became open to receiving a child's love; then and only then could I receive what a child has to offer, and it is then that I deserved the love a child.

One-Liner: If you have the love of a child, some might say you have it all.

{ 8 }

A New Box of Crayons...

...my friend, who is a teacher, and I were on the phone once talking about the school supplies she was buying for her job. At the time, she was working for an institute for the intellectually challenged. That particular day, she was also buying one of her students a birthday present. They were not allowed to get this particular student anything that could double as a weapon of any kind because of his extreme aggression. Suddenly, I heard her gasp on the other end of the phone. "A new box of crayons!" she exclaimed. "I love new boxes of crayons!" She went on to say how pretty the colors were and how neatly they were all arranged, sharpened, and ready to use.

I suppose we all have memories of new boxes of crayons. Or at least I hope everyone does because everyone should. I mean, crayons aren't just sticks of colored wax. They are colorful. The bigger the box, the more colors there are. They are orderly. Pristine rows of unimagined potential. They are sharpened, just waiting to be used. For they are the vessels from which all uninhibited creativity flows. A green sky. A pink cow. A purple tree. When else in your life are you allowed, and hopefully encouraged, to be so creative, not yet bound by the rules of adulthood?

Society does not take the necessary time, in my opinion, to celebrate creativity, especially creativity in young people. Perhaps that's why piercings and tattoos are all the rage with the younger generations. Piercings, tattoos, crayons...they are all part of the same process of self-expression. If you think I am joking, do me a favor. The next time you see a young person with a tattoo, ask them about it. My guess? You'll get a profoundly meaningful response if you are able to refrain from judgment before you ask. For example, if you asked my stepbrother about one of his tattoos, particularly the one on his shoulder, he'd tell you it was borne out of his grief after his brother died by suicide.

One-Liner: Try thinking of each day like a new box of crayons: orderly, neat, colorful, and so full of potential. The colors you choose and the decisions you make are yours and yours alone. What colors will you choose to color your day? Imagine the possibilities.

{ 9 }

Gifts or Artistry...

...I was talking to one of my friends a while back, and the subject of being an artist came up. He was purporting that he was an artist or that something he was doing was an "art." My comment to him was something like, "You're not tortured enough to be an artist." To which he replied, quite aptly, "You don't have to be tortured to be an artist." And I thought, or do you?

He started talking about athletes, teachers, and other professions he saw as forms of art. And I said, "No. To me, those are gifts." I think everyone has a gift, or gifts if they are lucky. We just need to figure out what ours are. For some, that's very natural and instinctive. For others, it's a journey of self-discovery. In therapy, for example, that is something I will focus on from time to time, especially with clients in some sort of existential crisis (i.e., what does it all mean? Why am I here?) It is those clients who I believe just haven't found or cultivated their gifts yet. To me, a gift is something you are good at, naturally. You don't have to work hard at it; it comes relatively early and easily in your life. These days, some might refer to their gifts as their "superpowers!" In my experience, those who have not taken the time to realize and embrace their gifts/superpowers are usually those who express the most emptiness and lack of direction in their lives.

I have two gifts. In no particular order, they are connecting with people, despite being quite introverted, and expressing my thoughts using the written word. Obviously, connecting with people made being a psychologist an easy choice for me. Being shy and having bouts of mental illness has turned me into a writer. Let me take this one step further.

I think it is our gifts, and our lives based on those gifts, that choose us, not the other way around. For example, I don't have a choice but to write. A painter? A musician? It seems to me that they have no choice but to create.

One-Liner: Find your gifts. Try to find them early. Then develop them, cultivate them, enjoy them, and parlay them into your livelihood if you can, but most importantly, don't ignore them. We have this one life to live (that we know of), and we shouldn't squander a single bit of those gifts. That's the very definition of a life well lived.

{ 10 }

"Cause I Ain't Got No Color..."

...turns out, third-year medical students do lots of "rotations," and this particular client of mine was rotating through psychiatry when she told me this story.

She was doing rounds in an inpatient psychiatry unit when she came across one of the patients sitting in his room, playing with his feces. Turns out he was painting on the wall with it. When she appropriately asked him why he was doing this, he replied, "Cause I ain't got no color." If you ask me, given his resources, he was making the most of what he had. Seems that even mental illness can clear the cobwebs of our minds and let our own creativity shine through.

One-Liner: The profundities of life are often in the most obscure and least likely places. If your mind is truly open, there are opportunities to learn everywhere. Whatever you do in this life, never, ever close your mind; it may be the last door you'll ever close.

{ 11 }

A Letter to the Lost...

...one of the therapeutic techniques I use, as mentioned previously, is for my clients to write a letter to the person they've lost in their lives. Whether it's an intimate relationship, a parent, a friend who could not give you what you needed because of their own mental health issues, or a child, there is something healthy about writing one's thoughts and feelings down as if you could say them to the person.

Letters like these rarely get sent. I've written a few of my own. I wrote one just before I wrote this chapter, and as with most things I ask of my clients, I don't ask them to do things I haven't done. Since my hope is that this book helps people, and most of it reveals my soul as part of that effort, I thought about including the letter I wrote after the ending of a relationship. But seeing as this was a while ago and not relevant in my life anymore because of the healing I have done, I will omit it, but I do not want my lack of an example to be a deterrent to you writing your own letter to heal.

So, please, write your letters. There might be one. There might be a few. Mail it...don't mail it...email it...keep it to yourself...text it...burn it...dissolve it in water, and flush it. Or don't do any of those things. But above all else, do it for yourself, not for its intended receiver. The goal of any grief work I do, which, by the way, is probably the most difficult work anyone will do, is accepting that the person is no longer part of your life. With acceptance comes embracing the fact that we do not control everything in our life, and the minute you embrace that fact is the minute you can start living, in the truest sense of the word, learning from those we've lost, being open to the lessons they have to teach us; and learning to live in a world where control is an illusion.

Please do yourself a favor. Mourn. Grieve. Embrace and live through the loss. Your heart will heal. If you do it right, grieve, that is, your heart will heal. It may be scarred, but it might be even stronger in some places. It will forever be different, but it will still work the same. If you haven't dealt with all of your losses, sometimes they come back when you least expect it and you must deal with several at once. This becomes difficult or complicated bereavement. Fear not. It might just take a little longer, but the process must be respected and trusted. Find your voice. Let yourself heal. Let yourself live.

One-Liner: A letter is only one way to begin the grieving process. There are many, and you must find what works for you. Remember: Do it for yourself, start living with peace now, and embrace the time you had with this individual rather than lament all the things you didn't have with this person. As they say, be happy that it happened, not sad that it is over. This can be very, very difficult. A letter is a step in the right direction.

{ 12 }

I Don't Have a Choice, Really…

…I remember learning about free will in school. Years ago, I committed myself to the existential philosophy of searching for my own life's meaning with the understanding that life is inherently meaningless. So, of course, to make my own choices would mean living a life that I choose, good or bad, and living with those choices. It's not just the old adage, "Life is what you make it," as much as it is that life is a series of choices, your choices, and your ability to make the best choices at any given moment in time. It is those choices, then, that give your life meaning. I believe it's much deeper than that, and by "it," I mean one's journey to a meaningful life.

For those interested in examining this further, I reference the book *A Man's Search for Meaning* by Victor Frankl. It is an exceptional book, life-changing for me, about a Jewish man during the Holocaust who seemingly arbitrarily escaped the gas chamber in Nazi Germany numerous times during World War II while his family was not so "lucky." He then is left alone with a lifetime of wondering why he was repeatedly spared, and those he loved were not.

So, my life has been full of choices that have taken me around the world, around the United States, back to my home state in the Midwest, and now in the South, where I currently live. It's been quite a journey indeed, and it's not nearly over. I digress.

Choices. When I was thirteen, I decided to be a psychologist because of what my mother went through after her divorce from my father. I wanted to help women like my mom live their best lives...children...financial independence...and never depend on a man for money. I went straight through college and graduate school without ever questioning that decision. My whole life's goal has been to be financially independent enough, so I would not rely on a man (or anyone for that matter) to provide for me. Funny how that single decision would come to dictate my life of thirty-something years, and it still does today to some degree. Mind you, though, it's not so that I would have enough money to support myself, but that I would have enough money to take care of my family as they move into their older years.

Choices. I was speaking with a friend a while ago. She had just seen the movie *Monster* (with Charlize Theron starring as the executed female serial killer Aileen Wuornos, which turned out to be an Academy Award-winning performance). She was clearly disturbed by the film, which I have since seen and thoroughly enjoyed, or enjoyed as much as one can enjoy a film about a prostitute turned serial killer. At one point in the film, Aileen, evidently called "Lee" in her real life, is sitting at a bar speaking to Bruce Dern's character, who ultimately knows that she is the one killing all of these "johns." She says to him, knowing that he knows she is the wanted killer, that she doesn't have a choice but to kill these men.

I believe Jeffrey Dahmer would probably have said the same thing. This is the pivotal point in the film, and one I feel parallels my own life. This may sound odd, but there have been points in my life that I did not choose certain things; rather they chose me. And remember, up to this point in my life, free will has been an unshakable tenet.

Psychology. I fought tooth and nail in graduate school, and through my pre-doctoral internship, I realized that I did not ever want to "practice" psychology. I didn't want to see clients. I was convinced none of them ever got better. I was convinced the downfall of psychology as a field was going to be the schism that exists between the science and practice of psychology. And then, along came this thing called the "job market." I was unable to secure a job doing research or some application thereof. The next thing I knew, I was back in my home state, where the only job available was a clinical one. So, I took it, started seeing clients, got licensed, and ten years later, I am still practicing psychology. I'm good at it; people respond to me; my approach to helping people appears well-received by both my clients and colleagues. Did I choose the field of psychology? Yes. Did I ever, in a million years, think I'd be a successful practitioner in the field? Absolutely not, but it was one of my gifts, and I took advantage of that.

Writing. I can honestly say, when I look deep into my soul, that writing has chosen me. I was shy, quiet, and extremely introverted growing up. The only way for me to get out of my head as a child was to write. I can tell you that after thirty-plus years of staying quiet, I finally have something to say. And not just to those around me but to a bigger audience, the biggest audience. In fact, I have so much to say that I am almost helpless to the voices in my head. Couple that with my unending ambition and desire to be financially successful, and you will have the makings of a true, successful, soul-fulfilling writer. Did I choose to be a writer? Definitely not. Did it choose me? Do I have any other choice but to tell my story? I'm afraid I don't, and I won't stop writing until I have nothing left to say, which is unlikely but not out of the realm of possibilities. I'm not sure what is next, but I can tell you my writing is purposeful and meaningful and gives me an enormous amount of peace. I believe it to be my obligation to be open to it and receive it as a gift.

PEARLS AND PURSE STRAPS... OR HOW A SHRINK "SHRINKS" HERSELF

One-Liner: Whether you believe in a deterministic world or one of free will, promise yourself that you will still make choices, for they may be the exact choices you were meant to make; the reasoning may be circular, but you are neither a victim, for that is a choice, nor a passive participant in a pre-determined world.

{ 13 }

The Colors That You Choose to Paint Your Day...

...mine are pretty shitty today. Crappy colors today. I chose them, or did I? Maybe they chose me? I suppose it's good I'm not painting with shit today.

So, I'm in this on-again, off-again relationship, which has caused me great pain, but yet my heart still belongs to him. I happen to be of the mindset that we don't choose who we love; we choose who we marry, have a family with, etc., but not who we love. If we did, I would have left the relationship long ago. I promised myself a while back that I would not let him hurt me again, that I wouldn't care if we stayed in a relationship or not. But here I sit. Hurt. Sad. Angry. And those are the colors I chose to paint my day today.

That line reminds me of a song on the soundtrack from the movie *Jerry Maguire*. It is true that we choose the colors of our days. The good news is I can choose different colors tomorrow...if I want to. And the other good news is I choose the colors, no one else. If I'm mad, hurt, sad, or happy, I will choose those colors because that's where I am at this moment. And, perhaps more importantly, I am okay with that. Tomorrow is a new day. Tomorrow is a different day, a different palette. I can choose the same colors every day for a week, a month, a year, or even a lifetime if I am so inclined. We all know people who paint their days with the same colors, day in and day out. There are those who might even tell you they are victims of their colors. Me, I choose not to be a victim. My colors may be shitty today and even tomorrow, but I will live to choose different colors.

This brings to mind another quote I like that reads: "Courage doesn't always roar. Sometimes courage is the quiet voice at the end of the day that says, I will try again tomorrow." I don't know what color courage is. I don't know what color "trying again" is. But I do know that I will get up tomorrow and choose. Even if my colors are shitty again, they are my choices.

One-Liner: Every single day, the colors you choose to paint your day are yours and no one else's; maybe even free will has a color; who knows? So, find your colors each and every day, and be glad that you are able to do so.

{ 14 }

Sex or Pain...

...I'm thinking about suffering. And I don't mean like I'm trying to decide if I want to suffer. I mean, I'm wondering how many people really know what it is to suffer. Maybe more than I think. Maybe less than I think. Maybe some people have bad things happen to them but don't experience emotional pain. Maybe others suffer over small, inconsequential things. And then there are those of us who have pain in our soul, in our spirit, those to whom dying sometimes seems a better alternative.

Interestingly, suffering tends to put me in touch with God. Usually, it comes in the form of a question like, "Why me?" or bargaining, like, "I'll do anything to make it stop." Again, I believe we all get closer to God (whichever deity/universe to whom you pray) when we suffer. Are we really owed an explanation? Not really. Would it be nice if I understood why I have this pain in my soul? Yes.

What I do not possess is the ability to blindly accept my suffering without asking what purpose it serves. Some might say that is my problem, that I question too much and need to blindly accept. However, I believe in my heart that if there is a God, that God would not want us to blindly accept what S/He chooses for us. S/He gave us a brain and the ability to wonder why, and I suspect S/He expects us to use it. So, I go on suffering; I go on questioning. In a completely unselfish way, I want others to learn what it took me years to learn. Perhaps that's why I am a good psychologist. Not because I know what it is to suffer but because my suffering was meant to educate and help others.

So, you're asking what any of that has to do with sex. Before I address that, let me just say that for those of you who do see mental health practitioners for therapy or some type of emotional help, do me a favor. Try to make sure they, themselves, understand suffering because if they don't, I'm not sure they have any business mucking around in yours. Do I think psychologists have to have suffered personally to be good psychologists? No. Do I think that in order to be a great psychologist, you need to have suffered? I certainly think it helps. And by great, I mean, gifted-, creative-, insightful-, extraordinary-, and a contributor-in-the-field kind of psychologist. Don't settle for any less. I ask that you just trust me on this.

Back to sex...and pain, emotional pain that is. For some reason, I've been thinking of the movie *Monster's Ball* lately. An extraordinarily simple film. One I would recommend, and not just because Halle Berry brought home the Oscar for her performance, but because of one scene. I am speaking of the brutally explicit sex scene between Billy Bob Thornton's character and Berry's. I was speaking to a friend recently and he was commenting on how hard that scene was for him to watch. When I asked him why, he said it was because of Berry's character's extreme vulnerability at the time, having just lost her son, despite which the sex continued. Right then and there, I knew. I knew my friend had never truly suffered.

The scene, to me, made profound and perfect sense. She had been through an enormous amount of tragedy and loss. It seemed that her very survival was under constant threat. In my experience, when the psyche is under so much duress, the body and its sensory systems must take over. The transformation for her was such that she was willing to do anything, anything to her body so that it would distract her from the searing emotional pain. Sex is real; it's intense; you feel it in every sensory organ that you have. It may even hurt. If you're lucky, it will hurt when you need it to, and it will be pleasurable when you need it to. For only then does the physical pain comfort, soothe, distract, and ease the emotional pain.

One-Liner: Our bodies know just what to do when our psyches cannot take any more: we feel physical pain—we hurt ourselves, get excruciating back pain, get in a car accident, break a bone—you get the gist; our bodies know just when to distract us with physical pain; bruises, abrasions, or broken bones. The body heals; pain in your soul may or may not, but physical anything is better than psychological despair. Learn to recognize and differentiate between physical and emotional pain; this helps healing begin.

{ 15 }

"Do You Have an Ending Yet?"...

...A Comment On the Process...

...I can't tell you how many times I have heard this question from my mother. I didn't start writing fiction until I was in graduate school, getting my doctorate in clinical psychology. But once I started writing, I couldn't stop. I haven't stopped. I can't stop.

However, this is what troubles me. The second I tell my mother that I have started writing a new book, invariably, she replies, "Do you have an ending yet?" Though I have tried to explain to her that writing a book, not unlike painting a picture or creating a sculpture, is so much more about the process of writing or creating than it is the story or the content or "the ending" therein. She still doesn't seem to be able to understand this. Any creation is a work of art, the product of an artist's process, a part of the writer's soul. I think there are just some people who are all about the ending of something rather than the journey, to speak metaphorically. Certainly, I forgive her for that transgression. But, as a writer, it becomes somewhat difficult to stay true to your own process in the face of comments like these.

I just finished reading my local Sunday newspaper with my dogs lying around me, a ritual that has become a slight indulgence. An article appeared by a local writer discussing the process of writing and emphasizing that the ending eludes most writers who start a novel from the beginning. I can tell you that, for me, those books or ideas that come to me in complete form, including the ending, most often get written as screenplays rather than novels. With a screenplay being much more formulaic than a novel, the structure and the system of creating a screenplay work well for me. But a novel? That is an entirely different process. When I use the word *process,* I mean sharing my soul, which, by the way, speaks to why I am not open to content changes when it comes time to edit one of my fictional works. To me, that would be like saying to Picasso, *go back and repaint part of a painting to make the message or expression clearer.* I hope that, like any truly committed artist, he would say "no" for the sake of preserving the integrity of his art in its purest, rawest form. Art is so much more than the content of the finished product. To the artist, it is the soul-searching, heart-wrenching process of creating that is the art itself.

There are people out there who need endings. The reality is I don't know how my stories will end. I don't know how my life will end. All I can do is comment on the process along the way. I don't even know how any particular chapter will end, both metaphorically in my life and literally in my books. The difference between people like this and me is that I embrace the ambiguity of the process, the unknowns of life. That, to me, is what content living is all about: embracing the fact that we don't know how things are going to end. We don't know what happens when it's over. We don't know where the process will take us. The alternative is either a life-long struggle against trusting the process by making plans and not letting life happen to you or enjoying the unpredictable process that is life. So, I say revel in the process; be about the process of the journey.

One-Liner: As in life, a good book will write its own ending; that is what I call "the process," and I trust it explicitly.

{ 16 }

Souls On Board...

...my stepfather is a pilot. One day, I happened to be looking over his shoulder while he was filing a flight plan. I noticed that one of the questions asked for the "number of souls" that would be on board. I don't know if this is still a question on flight plans, but at that time, this question was particularly poignant to me given I have always struggled to understand the concept of a soul, what it is exactly, and more specifically, what happens to that part of us when we die.

The questions on the flight plan did not specify or make a distinction between what types of souls were on board, just the quantity. We often flew with our dogs, so I wondered if their souls were counted. I finally asked my stepfather if the flight plan included that question so that they would know how many bodies to look for if we crashed. I think he answered me with a mumbled, "I guess so," as if to suggest he had never really put much thought into it. His answer, of course, left me completely, spiritually unsatisfied.

Just the other day, he was flying me back to where I was living after visiting my hometown, and I asked him if he counted the dogs that traveled with us among the "souls on board." A little more responsive this time, he said, "No," but clarified that he could write it somewhere else on the flight plan that we had dogs on board.

This notion of souls on board was meaningful to me. How many souls do I have on board my "plane?" How many people do you have on your plane? How many people would they have to look for if you crashed? How many people have gotten on and off your plane in your lifetime? How many souls do you have in your life who would come looking for you if your plane went down? Me, I have maybe a dozen who would come looking, but only about two or three who are actually on board with me.

I feel lucky to have them aboard my plane. Those select two or three would do anything for me, and I would do anything for them, which is why they are on my plane. No matter what. No questions asked. That's what I mean by souls on board.

Take stock of the souls aboard your plane. Are they good people? Not malicious in any way? Are they positive forces in your life? Are you getting as much out of the relationships as you are putting into them? Maybe it's time to lighten the load and get rid of excess baggage that's weighing you down or holding you back from being the best person you can be.

Despite the decisions you make regarding any dead weight you're hauling around, always know this: Exactly how many souls do you have on board your plane, and what would you do or not do to keep them there and why? After all, if the plane is going down, you need someone you can rely on to count and look for the number of souls lost. People who know me would know to look for my dogs, so I guess maybe it doesn't matter if they get counted in the final tally or not.

We take many flights in our life. We have different souls aboard different routes. My stepfather's plane has six seats. While this is hardly population control, I feel better knowing only five other souls, at most, plus or minus the dogs, can be lost at any given time in his plane.

One-Liner: A soul count is essentially an existential roster for those who fly: an existential headcount if you will. It simplifies the process should that day on the plane be your last. Make sure you are surrounded by your carefully chosen souls on all of your flights; God forbid any of them should be your last.

{ 17 }

Moments...

...we'll stick to aviation analogies for a second. My stepfather has been known to say that flying is "hours and hours of utter boredom interrupted by moments of sheer terror." I wonder, too, if this can be analogous to life. At times, life just passes us by for years at a time without any real difficulties or moments, good or bad. Today, however, I had a moment. Mine wasn't a moment of terror, mind you, but rather one of connectedness.

I don't believe that, as human beings, our lives change or are dictated by any one or two single moments. Rather, who we are as people is ultimately defined by the moments we have and how we handle them. It was unique, this moment today because it was a moment shared with a coworker; it was a moment of connectedness. He looked at me, and I looked at him. For a split second or two, there was a mutual moment of understanding, of empathy, of peace. We didn't speak of it, and we probably never will. But that's okay because a moment defines itself.

Keep in mind that my mantra for the first three-quarters of my life was, "We are all in this alone." I actively embraced the idea that we were each rowing our own boat amid a sea of other fledgling vessels doing the same. We can't really help each other as much as we can just stay in our own boat and watch helplessly as others learn to sink or swim.

But now, many years of maturity and wisdom later, I do see all of us as intertwined, interwoven, interdependent, and interconnected. And from time to time, we get a glimpse of that. It's a glimpse, sometimes just a flash, which comes with the realization we are in this together, that we can help each other, that we can reach out to one another. You may never get someone to accept your hand, as for some of us it is challenging to ask or receive help. But as long as you are willing to keep reaching, someone will grab hold of you and the two of you can pull each other to safety. The person reaching back probably won't be who you'd expect it to be; it might be the person you least expected, which makes it all the sweeter.

Be who you are and embrace those defining, rare, beautiful moments of connectedness. Hopefully, they won't be full of terror. There are thousands and thousands of people in the world with whom you have hundreds of interactions, but only a few will be moments of connection. Those will be moments when time stands still and the world stops. Just for a second, everything stops. Cherish those moments; treasure them. They do not happen very often, so we must receive the peace they give us.

One-Liner: Strung together, these moments are what create happiness; what's the secret to happiness? No such thing, silly; if you are paying attention, life will give you moments of complete joy, connectedness, and happiness. You must be ready to receive them when you are lucky enough to have them: that is true happiness.

{ 18 }

Not Now...

...I am so not ready for my parents to die, or even be sick, or even get older. I'm not sure I understand why this needs to happen. I mean, sure, we all get older. It's the cycle of life. I get it. I understand that. But losing our parents? No. Not yet. Not now. Not today. It's not fair. It's not right. It's not going to happen.

We call that a healthy dose of denial in the circles I run in. Of course, I know my parents will die. Maybe I'll have a family of my own by then. I just pray to God that when it happens, I will be financially independent enough not to have to work after either of them dies. I have had emotional breaks, and by breaks, I mean breaks with reality, including at least one for which I probably should have been hospitalized. I know it's coming, a breakdown when I lose my mother or father; I just pray it's not in front of my staff or colleagues. It probably should be because what could be more supportive than a group of mental health workers? But I prefer to have my breakdowns in the privacy of my own head.

If I don't have children or a husband, I don't know who will take care of me once my parents die. I mean, I know how to take care of myself. I've been doing it for a while now. It's just that I've seen the edge of sanity and come back a couple of times; I worry that if I see it again, I may not come back.

I sit here and think about my dad lying in a hospital, as he did several years ago, his body cold, with forty pounds of water weight on him and a fifty percent chance of living, I am overwhelmed with sadness. No one or nothing could have prepared me for that. When the chaplain of the hospital meets you off the elevator and asks you to accompany him to see your father for perhaps the last time, it's a surreal experience. Reading my father's last rites as we all prayed, holding hands around him, was something I never wanted to experience again. He did survive; he is alive as I write this. But will I ever be ready for one of my parents to die? Probably not. Was experiencing him being sick a life-altering experience that changed me forever? Yes. I can honestly say that, to this day, nothing matters to me but the health and well-being of the people I care about. If, at the end of the day, all those people are alive and healthy, no matter the condition, that's a good day.

When God decides to start taking people from me, and S/He will, I hope S/He also gives me the strength to survive. No one ever teaches you how to survive a death like that. I do grief counseling all the time, and each time, I must watch my empathy level as grief strikes at the core of my being. It's almost like I have been grieving my entire life. For what, I have no idea. Perhaps it has made me stronger. Perhaps my losses up to this point in my life have been preparatory for the inevitable. Maybe I'll surprise myself with inner strength. Or maybe I'll be back at the edge of sanity and fall the other way. No matter how or when it happens, I can say I have lived my life *always* letting those in it know how I feel about them. Tomorrow, no one is promised.

One-Liner: Since I wrote this chapter a few years ago, my father has passed, and I am married. I survived his loss. I do believe he did the best he could for me and my brother despite his own emotional challenges. The message of this chapter, however, stays the same: Say what you gotta say to those you gotta say it to, and then you might at least live without regret, even if you are not prepared for the unfortunate grief that follows losing one of those you love.

One of the ways I cope with loss, ironically, is my work. It seems to usually happen that way: all of the clients being assigned to me are also dealing with loss and grief. By helping them through their grief, I process my own, crying with them, writing with them, and having counseling with them. These are the very things that I needed while helping them. When my sadness was peaking, nearly every assigned client was dealing with some type of loss. In keeping with my therapeutic style, transparency is the number one rule. For each client who expressed "grief" as their presenting issue, as part of the first session, I would invariably tell them that I was grieving my own loss. Doing so usually increased my empathy for them, theirs for me, and was an overall benefit to the therapeutic alliance and process of therapy itself. After all, I am first human before I am a psychologist.

{ 19 }

Stand Up Eight...

...inspiration comes at the oddest times, whether you are looking for it or not. So, I was sitting on the floor in Target one day, trying to pick out a greeting card. Having so many things in my arms, rather than getting a cart, I just sat down right in the middle of the aisle. As an aside, not getting a cart is my way of doing damage control. That way, I can only buy what I can fit in a hand-held basket. While I was sitting there, surrounded by my purchases, a particular greeting card caught my eye. "Stand Up Eight," it read. I grabbed it, opened it, and read the inside of the card. "Fall seven times, stand up eight," it read. Right in the middle of Target at about nine p.m. on a Friday night, I had a moment of clarity. For a few seconds, the world made sense. The card, or its saying, didn't give me riches or wealth. Because if it had, I wouldn't have been turned down for a Target credit card that very night because my credit was so bad. But the epiphany: priceless.

For some reason, this card struck me as both a writer and as a person. As a writer, I found out fairly quickly that I had to become good friends with rejection. I learned to expect it. I learned to embrace it. In the writing business, rejection or criticism must become meaningless. As with most writers, you write for one person and one person only. Yourself.

Rejection, both personally and professionally, needs to be put into perspective. Rejection is one person's opinion of you or your work on one particular day or at one particular moment in their life. In any situation, we cannot let rejection define us. We cannot let it win. I don't care if it's the seventh time or the thousandth time, we have to keep standing up. If *you* believe in yourself and your work, all you have to do is stand one more time than you fall. I believe that is the definition of perseverance.

How you handle your disappointments and your failures will define you as a human being, not how you handle success. Anyone can handle success.

One-Liner: To accept and completely embrace failure is to stand up the eighth time; stand up one more time than you fall; that is what defines you.

{ 20 }

Poodle Nightmares and Other Challenges...

...for those of you who don't know me, which is hopefully a lot, at the time I wrote this chapter, I had two dogs (no children, but then the difference still remains somewhat elusive). I have two Standard Poodles (capitalization mine...and for the rest of this book...reflecting my respect for the breed). For all intents and purposes, they are my children. I was lying on the bed, and they were both on either side of me. Suddenly, one of them started to cry in her sleep.

She started twitching, paws moving, tail wagging, and continuing to cry. I tried to wake her, but I couldn't. I said her name, but she kept crying and twitching. I touched and shook her, but she continued to howl. Finally, I kissed her on her face and made loud sounds until she awoke. She opened her little eyes and looked at me as I continued to kiss her. She stretched and yawned, laid her head back down, sighed the poodle sigh, then closed her eyes again. I laid back down and thought, "Ah, poodle nightmares. I wonder what they dream about."

For some reason, this makes me think about having babies or introducing another challenge in my life. When does one know it is the right time to, say, get married or have babies? I mean, a partner for life? Having children for life? Commitments like that...how does that work? Timing? Luck? How does the universe come together in a singular moment to help you make these timely decisions?

Really, all I need is to be loved enough by someone who will wake me from those horrible nightmares. It doesn't seem like such a big ask.

One-Liner: We all need someone to protect us—even from ourselves, or at least to kiss us awake from our deep, disturbing nightmares. That's all. As for the rest of it—the partner, the soulmate, children, dogs—I might just let the Universe decide those things for me.

{ 21 }

A Perfect Day for Rain...

...it was a perfect day to die. Somehow, the rain seemed appropriate. It made it okay. Maybe it was a sign that today was the right day to die. I'm not much for signs, but rain, it's hard to ignore. My feet get wet. My hair gets wet. My clothes get soaked. The thunder and lightning are added treats. A bit more dramatic, they make it. The cleansing. There's something pure about the rain. If I let it bathe me, I suppose it could. But my soul. I don't think it could cleanse my soul. Only death can do that. Only death can bring peace to my soul. Bring it to rest. The rain can clean my body. Death can clean my soul. But, the rain, the rain makes it a perfect day to die.

One-Liner: I used to have days when I would have to go help people when it felt like all I really wanted to do was die; awful, those days, it turns out helping others was exactly what I needed to help myself. (Pause to let that sink in—it turns out helping others can be the best way to help ourselves.)

{ 22 }

College Football & Other Choices...

...OK, let's change head spaces. I think it's time.

ION (in other news)...I love college football. I love watching college football. I love going to the games, the smell in the air, the changing of the seasons, the competition, and the young men who dedicate the collegiate years of their lives to the sport. Say what you will, but there is something about the physical and mental dedication these men have and use to become the best athletes they can be. I find it inspiring.

During one of my hard-fought nights of painful sleep, I was on social media in the middle of the night. As I was scrolling my social media feeds, I came across a photo of Ezekiel Elliott. I remember watching him play at Ohio State as a stand-out wide receiver/running back. I remember seeing him on the sidelines with what I thought was a crazy hairdo. Watching him play, I remember thinking that he was special. Sure enough, he was drafted and went on to a successful career in the National Football League.

One-half of the side-by-side photo I had seen was his look while at Ohio State. The other half was his NFL "look." Sure enough, in his NFL photo, gone was his crazy hair and unkempt beard to match. It was as if, overnight, he went from a kid playing touch football in the backyard to a man playing in the big leagues. He looked even more special. His hair groomed; his beard manicured; it somehow seemed to soften him.

Upon sharing this photo comparison with my husband, he remarked that "Zeke" was in the sports news recently for some things he had allegedly done...bad things. But he looked so grown-up like the NFL had turned him into a gentle, confident man. Unfortunately, the news shared a potentially different side of Mr. Elliott.

What I love about watching college football is how hard the young men, just out of high school, work. They are at perhaps their peak physically and work so hard to maintain their bodies and get better with each season. Their bodies are like elite machines. Their minds are focused. They almost never make the same mistake twice if they are well-coached. I find them to be special, hard-working individuals who provide undeniable entertainment every Saturday for their die-hard fans. Watching what they put their young bodies and minds through every weekend for my entertainment and a billion-dollar industry is inspiring. (As a side note, they were only recently given the benefit of profiting from the use of their "Name, Image, and Likeness" as college students. Sometimes, I think I liked it better when they played out of sheer love of the game.)

I believe college athletes are using the very specific gifts they were given to show us what greatness looks like in a 20-year-old man. And I will continue to remember what Ezekiel Elliott did for the football program at The Ohio State University™. I do not ignore, condemn or support the alleged activities that go on in his private life. Instead, I choose to enjoy my Saturday afternoons, watching in awe of the greatness.

One-Liner: The only difference between college athletes and us is that their life decisions make headlines. Ours don't. Is that a reason to stop watching and supporting collegiate football? For some, yes. For me, no. No matter who it is I'm watching every Saturday afternoon, I will continue to watch. Eddie George, Ezekiel Elliott, Justin Fields, and Marvin Harrison, Jr. are all examples of elite bodies and minds that were driven to be the best in college football.

{ 23 }

My First Suicide...

...I was home in Ohio on my first holiday break from graduate school in Palo Alto, California. The year was 1991, I believe. I was sleeping in my old room on Christmas evening. I was awakened in the middle of the night by my mother. I'm not sure why, but I was irritated and aggravated upon being woken.

"What?!" I asked my mother.

"Tony shot himself," she replied.

I woke all the way and responded, "Oh my God."

I don't remember much of that break other than two things: the funeral and dropping off my stepfather at the house he owned and was renting to his two adopted sons. They were eighteen and nineteen years old at the time, I believe. There were other men living there, and it was obvious a party had recently occurred there. One of the young men was going through a breakup with his girlfriend, and he had somehow managed to lock himself in a room with a weapon. The others heard the gunshot and broke into his room to find him dead. The next day, I took my stepfather to the house "to clean up the mess." It was a heartbreaking day.

A father having to clean up "the mess" his dead son had left behind after taking his own life. Never, ever should this have to happen. But there I was, dropping him off with a bucket and a mop.

I cried through the entire funeral. Uncontrollably at times. I didn't know him very well because his dad had only just married my mom a few years before. I had lived with him briefly before he went off to the military. Having had some trouble there, he returned home. He and his biological brother were close. My stepfather had adopted four kids, three "birth siblings," two brothers and a sister, along with a fourteen-year-old, non-related girl. When he was divorced, he got custody of all four kids.

My mom having married into this family, I don't ever remember being asked if I cared if they moved into my home, but in they came. It was sort of a blurry time in my life, looking back. I was in school to become a psychologist when he died. I remember his friends all got tattoos to remember him. It was the beginning of my graduate career; it was the first suicide I had been close to, and it was the beginning of my own mental health problems. Coincidence? I doubt it.

One-Liner: No parent should ever have to deal with the loss of a child, especially one who died by suicide, ever. The National Suicide Prevention Lifeline is now a three-digit number. For those in distress, dial 988 for help.

{ 24 }

Sometimes, a Closed Door is Just a Closed Door...

...a quiet word to introverts.

One-Liner: This goes out to all the introverts. There is no chapter to explain how being an introvert has affected me. To the rest of the extroverted world: Please don't judge introverts as being "aloof" or "off-putting"; let people be people; let people be who they are; don't make them keep their door open. Any room I'm in is my safe place; my job takes most of the friendliness out of me, unfortunately. I have a lot to say, clearly as evidenced in this book; I just don't want to talk about it! In fact, you introverts, you don't need to talk about it. It's okay to be yourself, to be different, and even more importantly, to honor and protect yourself from the expectations of others.

{ 25 }

Exquisite Pain...

...I don't suppose those words go together in sentences very often, if ever. For some reason, when I experience pain, it is exquisite. It's really the only word that comes to my mind. Most people have experience with pain. But I'm talking about pain that, for a second, stops you in your tracks. You can still walk; you can still move; the doctors tell you nothing is wrong with you. But there it is.

The tears start. The helplessness sets in. Hopelessness sets in. It feels like no one can help you. If you are lucky, you have a doctor who believes you and helps you relieve the pain. If you are lucky, you have a doctor who will give you handicapped parking paperwork to turn in at work. And all you can do is submit to the pain.

I've had migraines most of my life. I know about pain. The kind that induces uncontrolled vomiting, trips to the emergency room, IVs of anti-nausea medication, and narcotic pain relievers. That's the pain I know. It is exquisite as well. Thank you, God, or whomever, for allowing doctors to be smart enough to create new, effective medications. I used to have to give myself a shot of medication to stop the pain. People used to always say, "Doesn't it hurt, the shot?" And for those of us who know migraines, the pain of a needle pales in comparison to the pain going through my head. However, the pain of which I speak in this chapter is not about migraines but about the pain the last two years have brought me.

It is a long story and one that isn't quite over as I write this. Below is the email I wrote to my family after the final discovery of what was wrong with me after a painful two-year illness:

2/2/17
All –
I've heard an expression that goes something like this, "Like everything else that sucks in my life, I did it to myself." This is in reference to the last (almost) two years of suffering with an undetermined illness. As I continued to research my symptoms, I decided to go back to when my symptoms first started. As it turns out, after Macy and Safina (my two dogs) passed, I became very ill, as some of you might remember, and the doctors started me on two additional medications, one for back/neck spasms, and one for anxiety. This was February 2015. Sure enough, (mother does know best, by the way), I recently researched both of those medications that were started at that time, and under "very rare" side effects of one were joint pain and weight gain, and the other had gastroparesis (when your stomach stops digesting food) as a "very rare" side effect. I stopped both of those medications immediately, with a little weaning, and am happy to report that I am virtually pain-free, walking for exercise, and feeling so much better. I am slowly beginning to feel that my body is mine again. I feel that the weight is slowly starting to come off as well. I do not weigh myself, so I just go by how my clothes fit. My gastrointestinal system is starting to work again, slowly, as I get hungry now again. With caution, I am optimistic that I will continue to get better. I think I had a medication-induced rheumatologic condition, which I (on the advice of doctors at the time) created by introducing these new medications two years ago. Yes, I did it to myself! I just wanted to thank everyone for your thoughts, prayers, and well wishes during those two years. (I will continue to take them as I, hopefully, recover from these last two awful years.)

Thank you again for your unconditional support and love.

Always,
Beth-Anne

To all who are suffering; to all who understand what is meant by "exquisite pain"; to all who believe we are smart enough to figure out what is wrong with us; to all who know the power of grief, please continue to believe that we were given the intellect to figure out what is wrong with us; and if we weren't—others were. But please take note: If a doctor tells you they don't know what is wrong with you, send you to a shrink because it *must* be psychosomatic if they can't figure it out, I say, "I'm sorry you're not able to figure out what is wrong with me. And if you were to admit that we'd be halfway to a cure by now." To those suffering, I won't say, "Hang in there," because there were multiple times that I nearly did not. There are still days I wonder if I can. It may well take me as long to heal as I suffered, maybe longer. My body knows. I know. You know. I just want you to know there are people who do understand exquisite pain.

One-Liner: Never give up finding the solution to a problem, especially one that involves your own body; if a doctor 1) tells you there is nothing wrong with you; 2) sends you to a shrink because it must be "in your head," or 3) doesn't trust you with a narcotic pain reliever; please know that 1) they have never actually experienced pain themselves; and 2) I'm sorry God didn't make them smart enough to figure out what is wrong with you...that's not your problem...find a different doctor!

{ 26 }

Gifts and Disabilities…

...we all have them. Some go to greater lengths to hide or display them. I believe that at the end of the day, we all have enormous gifts to offer to the world and to each other. Likewise, I believe that we are all disabled in some way. My gift is my time and empathy if you happen to be a client of mine. My disability is its own suffering.

We've talked about gifts and disabilities before, in the sense of creativity, work, and making sense of our lives. As not to repeat myself, I believe it all comes down to management and how you manage these forces in your life.

We all experience "teachable moments," as they say. I think what those really are are moments in which we can learn how to manage our own gifts and/or disabilities.

Gifts
People tell me I'm nice, friendly, and warm. Caring. Empathic. That one's a good one because I want people to see me as empathetic. I often have clients, the ones who are actually paying attention to me, tell me that they can see empathy in my eyes or on my face. I'm always surprised to hear this. Maybe they'll put that on my tombstone. *She was empathic and didn't even know it.*

A little background: In fifth grade, I won the science award for understanding the weather. In sixth grade, someone placed me in "Special Projects"—which meant I was put on a bus once a week with other kids and taken to a special learning place for gifted kids. I think I was one of three girls. I was in the honors program in undergraduate school and one of five Fellows in my major. I have a doctorate. Long before there was anything called STEM programs (Science, Technology, Engineering, and Mathematics) for young women, I had teachers recognize my abilities in math and science at an early age and ask me to be a Teaching and Research Assistant in college and graduate school. Recently, one person who knows me well described me in the following way to a mutual friend: "She's a genius, but a little quirky." Maybe they'll put that on my tombstone! Ha! I speak some Spanish. I used to think in Spanish. I would talk to my dogs in Spanish. That's a good gift, too.

Disabilities

This one might be a little bit easier. That's a terrible way to start! Teachable moment: Isn't that something...the bad things are always easier to enumerate than the good things...even when the evidence supporting the gifts outweighs that which supports the disabilities. Read: transparency is a good thing to embrace. I'll get to that later.

Well, maybe this won't be so hard. Depression. There it is. That's my disability. It is a disability. It is one that has enveloped, enraged, engrossed, and flat-out consumed my soul. Maybe that's another gift—hiding it. And maybe that is another one of my disabilities—*thinking* that I'm hiding it when people see right through me and know all of my deepest, darkest thoughts when they really cannot.

A little more, funnier history: At one of my last jobs, we had to bring in baby pictures, and people had to guess who was who based on the baby photos and then pick out the photo "with the cutest baby" or "the angriest baby...," etc. Not only did people know it was me in my photo, but I was picked as "the most serious baby." This was shocking to me. Not because I am not a very serious person, because I am—and apparently, that was evident to others from an early age. I didn't know others knew that about me! Or that anyone could garner that from a photograph!

Let me say it this way. Teachable moments, if we truly are paying attention, to me are things we need to learn to *manage* our own disabilities. When I am working with someone who has a chronic mental illness, I usually tell them that sometimes the best we can do is learn to manage our good or bad episodes. To manage a "bad" episode is to learn to be less intense and less frequent/minimize the time they cause distress, for example. Less intense and doesn't last as long because you have learned how to make this so. Is it a cure? No. It is an acknowledgment of your gifts and disabilities; acknowledge that you must manage them (i.e., with medication, change your cognitions, etc.) by controlling how long they last and how intense you let them get. It may not be a cure, but I guarantee it is a better way of life.

One-Liner: Embrace and celebrate your gifts; celebrate your disabilities...because I can guarantee they will fall under the opposite category at different times in your life. Learn to see "teachable moments" as ways the universe is trying to tell you how to "manage" them and hopefully live a more stable and emotionally managed life.

{ 27 }

The Power of Strangers or Why Therapy Works...

...in some ways, this might be the most difficult chapter for me to write. Let me give you a bit of context: It was January 2016. I was in the throes of my now-accurately-diagnosed illness (medication-induced lupus), and my doctor had taken me off all psychotropic medication (which I had been on in some form for twenty-plus years). My parents-in-law had just sold their water-side house, in which my husband and I were also living. We were moving, either them or ourselves, I cannot remember. I was driving into "town" from their house, which was about a thirty-minute drive. My car was full of stuff, probably not even mine at that point. I was alone. Typically, I am quite cautious about listening to music in my car, as it does intensify my melancholic mood more than it soothes me. I prefer to drive in silence. My radio was on and turned to NPR, a channel I do not listen to, which tells me that my husband was the last one to drive my car because he listens to National Public Radio quite a bit. For some reason, that day, I left it on because they were talking about mental health issues. I thought I would, or maybe should, listen. Boy, was that the wrong choice.

I was already crying, not quite into hysterics yet. I missed the beginning of the program, but there was a father talking about his mentally ill daughter. It sounded as if she had recently died, perhaps by suicide, the way he was crying and talking about her. He explained there was a night when she was young and in the house, crying and screaming. The father described how he was trying to comfort her. Apparently, she could not be comforted. He lost his patience and screamed at her, "Why are you doing this?" She looked at him through her tears and said, "Because I can't help it." And that, my dearest friends and family, is what mental illness is...because we cannot help it. He regretfully remembered that time in his daughter's life and expressed anger toward himself for not understanding. At this point, in the car, I was crying so hard as it occurred to me that my depression and anxiety had existed over the years because I simply couldn't help it. In retrospect, I should have pulled the car over because I was crying so hard, like driving in rain so dense you can't see what is in front of you. Listening to the father who was beside himself in grief, riddled with guilt, I found myself in a state of utter despondency and realization at the same time. Then...he started talking about therapy.

"... of course, my daughter went to therapists, lots of them," the father quipped. He then spoke of one therapist in particular. He remembered his daughter telling him how helpful therapy was, which rendered him feeling helpless and useless as a father. "If her own father can't help her and some stranger can, I must be failing as a dad!" he recalled thinking. Not only as a psychologist but as a person suffering from mental health issues myself, I was curious about where this part of the conversation was going. He said, "But then she told me, 'Dad, she is a stranger to me and has no interest in changing me as a human being. She has no investment in me becoming a different person, just in helping me.'" And there it was, why I do what I do.

In one emotionally terrifying moment, clarity struck. I couldn't pull myself together in the car, but, by God, this grieving father, as he cried through the interview, as he cried through his suffering and loss, so too did I. In that instant, I realized that when we are not invested in changing people as people, we are better able to help them. We divest ourselves from thinking they are going to become someone they are inherently not. Think of giving change to a homeless person on the street. Is that money going to change them as human beings, give them a job, or a home? Probably not. Is it going to temporarily get them a hot cup of coffee that will sustain them at that moment? Most likely, yes. When it is our parents, our children, our spouses, our partners, or our friends who suffer from mental illness, I think we somehow become emotionally invested in changing them or helping them as human beings. We are invested in making them better people. Mental health professionals? There is no investment in making anyone different from who they are. I help people get through personal issues and occasionally serious mental illness by accepting where they are, keeping them safe, and learning how to manage their emotional "disability." This is the power of therapy. We have always known that therapy works. We have never really known why. I believe this is why. Please, whether it's a homeless person in need or a mentally ill person in need, never underestimate the power of a stranger's kindness.

One-Liner: The less the investment in actual change, the more likely we are to accept a person as they are and not judge them or invest in them getting better. A father cannot do this; therefore, he cannot help but feel responsible for his daughter's continued mental health problems or her ultimate demise. I would tell him that he is not responsible. Mental illness is not there because she chose it. It's there because she cannot help it, and the only person who is going to help her is someone who is not directly or automatically invested in her growth or getting better. (Okay, that was multiple "liners," but each is as important as the other. This may be the most important chapter in this book.)

{ 28 }

Prince Charming & Sleeping Beauty, Really...

...who drops everything in the middle of their day to go to the pharmacy and get a prescription for you and bring it to you at work? My husband. As you know by now, I have a couple of medical ailments requiring medication, some "as needed" or PRN as we say in the medical field, most just once a month. I made the mistake of running out of my migraine medication and sitting at my job in a ridiculous amount of pain...in my brain. I need to use my brain for my job, so sitting in pain while I work only makes it hurt more.

I was able to get the pharmacy on the phone and get the "script" filled right away. The pharmacy texted me it was ready; I texted my husband it was ready; he texted me that he was on the way with the medication. Who does this? Apparently, my husband.

There are a lot of things he does wrong in our relationship. It's not perfect. We may or may not even be soulmates, whatever that means, but I will tell you what: he shows up for me when I need him most. I can tell you that *that* is why I married him. He has been the only man in my life, truly, who has shown up for me...that is, except for my stepdad, Phil; my doctor in Gainesville, Dr. Michael McTiernan; and my former boss, Jackie.

Back to my husband. It took me ten years, almost to the day, to realize he shows up for me, always. He makes me laugh when he drives me to work, which is one of my favorite times of the day. He packs my lunch, gets me to work as on time as I can be, and picks me up after work, which helps me end on time, too, at the end of the day. Because we don't have a lot of time together during the average work week, I look forward to our little trips in the car—about fifteen minutes each way to work, with the "Mouse" (my pet name for our Standard Poodle, Paisley) on my lap, the air conditioning blasting ("a cool blast" we call it since I seem to be stuck in perpetual menopause every morning), him yelling at traffic, me telling him to stop, him talking to me in different voices, mostly it's a man from the backwoods Bayou, and me laughing as I mentally prepare to go do a job that was my calling when I was a teenager. I usually get back in the car a different person, six clients, and nine hours later; he's usually in good spirits and genuinely tries to make me happy and laugh. Sometimes I'm having it, and sometimes I am not; sometimes he's in the mood, and sometimes he's not. Either way, the mouse is with him, and she insists on sitting on my lap (fifty-five pounds). We then take her to the park to let her run and go potty; then, it's back home for dinner, TV, and bedtime when we do it all over again.

The reason he may be my Prince Charming is that on the weekends, the routine differs. He gets up early, goes to Starbucks with the mouse to get me a "fluffy drink" and a little treat and to get her a "pup cup"—again, for those of you unfamiliar, this is a little cup full of whipped cream, free of charge, for dogs that come through the drive-thru. Since I am not in the car, this is their time together. He has the windows down for her to get fresh air, even when it is raining, and they have their morning ride together. I'm sure he talks to her and makes her laugh, too. Standard Poodles are generally considered one of the smartest dogs, usually second to Australian sheepdogs for those of you who don't know, and they have a sense of humor. Really. So, I'm sure she laughs at his shenanigans just like her mama does.

Stay with me... I'm getting to the fairy tale part... I promise.

I recently purchased a bedside table from Facebook marketplace, which is "big enough for eight people to play poker on," according to my husband. I have a lot of bedside needs. What can I say? Then, I usually put my oversized purse down by my oversized table and sleep in on the weekends. He comes to put my drink and treat on the table, but the more stuff I have around the bottom of the table, the more difficult it is for him to set the drink and treat down and lean over to kiss his "sleeping beauty" he calls me at these times. Therefore, that makes him Prince Charming—although he lacks his fair share of charm, don't get me wrong.

If I have to put up with moments of whatever the opposite of charm is, "unattractiveness" according to Siri, to get the other stuff out of the way, for him to show up for me as often as he does and with things I need to get through my day or weekend mornings, then he is my Prince Charming, and I am his Sleeping Beauty.

Please don't ever underestimate the value of people in your life who show up for you, whether your doctor of twenty years or your husband of five...for they truly are your Charming Princes (or Princesses) even if you don't always feel like you could possibly be someone's Sleeping Beauty, because everyone deserves to be someone's.

One-Liner: No matter who you are or what state you are in, people who show up for you—consistently and no matter what shape you are in or how much shit you have on or at the base of your poker-sized bedside table—are invaluable. So, remember, you have to clear a path, so to speak, and deal with your own shit so that your Prince Charming can get to you. You gotta get rid of the clutter so your Prince(ss) Charming can get to you. Who knows, s/he might even be your soulmate.

{ 29 }

Where Does the Sidewalk End…

…we were on our way to work this morning, my husband driving. He is almost always commenting on the traffic on our way to work. He has a particular issue with bikers on the road, especially if there aren't bike lanes for them. He was navigating a particular stretch of road this morning while passing a biker without a bike lane and commented about the sidewalk across the street. He said, "Wait 'til you see this, up here. The sidewalk just ends." He was right. On the other side of the road, where I assume he meant the biker could be safely biking and out of traffic, there was a sidewalk that ended after someone's lawn ended and did not continue down the street.

For some reason, his saying this took me immediately, in my head, to an image of me as a little girl, so shy, so quiet, so painfully alone, reading Shel Silverstein's book, *Where the Sidewalk Ends*. I remember that being one of my favorites as a child. I believe it was a book of poems. That book and *The Giving Tree* were two of my favorite books, and I've really only read one book as an adult that meant anything to me since. No, I take that back, there have been two. (But more on that another time.)

I have never been a reader, so that must have been a childhood thing for me. But I've always been alone. Alone with words. Just not others' words, necessarily. My words. I couldn't speak them, so

I wrote them. And for some reason, that memory came back strong this morning when he said ...where the sidewalk ends. And, even now, as I think about it, those are potent words for me, even as a child. a kid.

So...what does happen when the sidewalk ends? Do people stop walking? Do people keep walking just on something else? Asphalt. Grass. Concrete in another form. Certainly, the world doesn't end just because a sidewalk ends. Or does it?

I wonder what my thoughts were when I was just a child. I remember most of them. But I think the point today was sidewalks keep people safe. What happens when safety runs out? That's not a happy thought. But metaphorically, something must change when a sidewalk ends. Either the person traveling on it must change direction or traverse a different terrain. One, perhaps, safe. Less secure. People need to feel safe. Safe from other people. Other drivers. Themselves. And if the sidewalk must end, does it end safely? Or maybe that is just the universe telling us we must switch paths, or take some risks, or at least change directions, or find other ways of keeping ourselves safe.

What kept that little girl in her bedroom reading *Where the Sidewalk Ends* safe? She did, I suppose. I was given a bedroom to stay safe. Come to think of it, it was my sanctuary. Not unlike now, in a 4000+ square-foot home... I have carved out a safe 300-square-foot room that is my sanctuary. The door was always closed. Then and now. Not to keep me in but to keep others out. Out of my room, out of my thoughts, out of my space, out of my head. My thoughts have always been sacred to me. Now, they are becoming words that I write. Which makes them shared thoughts. Huh...when my sidewalk ended, I wrote. I wrote and wrote and wrote...and here we are!

If someone could have told that little girl in her Laura Ashley decorated, canopied bedroom, that she would be writing a book fifty years later, she might have believed them. What I wouldn't have believed was how many ended sidewalks I would have encountered along the way. Mr. Silverstein-was right all along. Where the sidewalk ends is not the end at all. It is the beginning of something. Something new. Something different. Something the whole world might someday read.

Don't get me started on *The Giving Tree*.

One-Liner: Your sidewalk may end abruptly or gradually; the question isn't why is it ending, but rather, what choices are you going to make when it does end...how or where will your travels...choices... or sidewalks...take you? Keep walking to find out... sidewalk or none.

{ 30 }

Mirrors...

...I just have one thought on this subject. Get rid of every single one out there. They have not served any productive purpose in my life, ever, I don't think. Someone will tell me if my clothes don't match. Someone will tell me if I have something in my teeth. Someone might compliment my outfit or my hair. That is how I will know how I look. The only thing that comes out of a mirror is a bad image of myself. Who needs that? Especially first thing in the morning or last thing at night. I don't. I avoid them at all costs.

It's almost as bad as having my photo taken. I think there is an old Native American saying that goes something like, "Every time I have a photo taken of myself, a piece of my soul dies." I feel that way looking into a mirror. I don't know why my husband loves me. I don't know why we live in a society that is so vain, we must see ourselves constantly. I don't. I just choose not to look. You can't un-see something you've already seen. So, why look? If that image is going to stay with me all day, then why look? I will invariably find something wrong with the image I see. So, God, let me get out the door in the morning without having to carry an image of myself all day.

People who see me during the day tend to comment on how confident I seem. And let me tell you, if they are getting that from me, it is completely projecting from within me. I must present myself differently than how I feel based on a mirror-image. Because whatever they are seeing is not what I see when I look in the mirror. Thank goodness I learned how to develop myself from the inside out.

One-Liner: Take time to develop who you are based on what you think you look like; know who you are, because if that image looking back at you isn't in agreement, whichever way it goes, it could ruin your whole day...or worse, your whole view of yourself—and yours is the only one that matters.

{ 31 }

A Life-Changing Day in Three Parts...

Part I: How to get over social phobia...

...gosh, this had to be about twenty years ago. As I previously mentioned The Ohio State University™ and my relationship to it was and is an integral part of my life. So, around the year 2000, I happened to be living in Columbus, Ohio. My father, a prominent attorney in Columbus, was an active member in the American Board of Trial Attorneys (ABOTA) association. At the time, I believe the president of ABOTA was a close friend of my father's and living in Columbus as well.

Lo and behold, along came their annual meeting. The meeting that year was something like a lovely brunch at a local attorney's even lovelier home on the beautiful Scioto River, followed by press box seats to the Ohio State football game that afternoon. My dad, may he rest in peace, was allowed a "plus one" to the event. Lo and behold, my father asked me to accompany him to this ABOTA event. Dreams *do* come true!

My father and I were enjoying brunch with all the trial attorneys (I'd say about one hundred) who were available and interested in either seeing this man's home or in having press box seats to an Ohio State football game. Being both, I was more than happy to tag along as my father's plus one. Anyway, we were enjoying delicious food, with interesting company, extraordinary views off the deck of this man's house, and then mayhem ensued.

As a backstory, my father was a man who enjoyed his alcohol. This was problematic throughout my life in various ways. As a child, it meant my dad would pick me up for visitation with a cup of vodka rocks in the cup holder. As an adult, it mostly meant me being the designated driver whenever I was with him.

The first thing my father did upon arriving at this event was to have a Bloody Mary. I stayed by his side mostly because I did not know anyone else there. And I was sober. There was also part of me that wanted to make sure he behaved, having spent most of my teenage years as the only sober female surrounded by drunken attorneys, God Help Me, and the misbehavior that accompanied, having to navigate that by myself. We headed to the buffet next.

We made our way through the line and re-entered the kitchen, where people were gathering. My father was proud to introduce me, his daughter, a clinical psychologist, with a doctorate and a license. Had I been less qualified, I'm not sure I would have even been allowed at this soiree. Standing in the kitchen, a full plate of food in one hand, and a Bloody Mary in the other, my father introduced me to one of the female justices of the Ohio Supreme Court.

My father was exceptionally charismatic, especially at events like this, using his litigation skills to hone his charm. In that instant, without warning, my dad dropped his entire plate of food on the Justice's feet, spilling it all over her, the floor of this immaculate kitchen, in front of at least fifteen-plus people, all well-known in the community. All I remember of that moment is seeing bright red marinara sauce on her feet. I could hear the collective gasp from the people in the kitchen. My father said something like, "Aw, shit," before he began his profuse apology to the Justice, followed by a huge helping of "mea culpa" with a side of a dozen paper towels to clean up the mess. All the while, my father was fussing over the Justice to help clean her up. To my recollection, I, at least, had the sense to set down my food and drink to help, desperately trying to make this less embarrassing for my father.

I don't know if the Bloody Mary had kicked in or if it was my dad's genuine apathy regarding the level of embarrassment that he had just brought upon himself, but he was able to keep the conversation moving and the party going without missing a beat. This, my friends, I believe, was the official end of my social phobia. Please allow me to explain.

Most of my life, including my childhood all the way to graduate school, I had this rather large monkey on my back. I was deathly afraid of being judged, scrutinized, and criticized by others, which translated to me being so quiet that in graduate school, a male classmate of mine asked me if I was mute. Whaaaat? I mean, sure, I cried before presentations; I couldn't raise my hand in class; I was nauseated at the thought of even just going around the classroom to introduce ourselves.

After therapy and ten years of growing up, here I was in potentially one of the most embarrassing situations I had been in in my life. Watching my dad handle himself, watching myself, watching him handle himself, and watching the Justice, watching him handle the situation were all, quite honestly, the simplest, most authentic, most genuine ways of being human. And having other human beings, despite their status in life, act with kindness and compassion and return the authenticity of the moment to reduce us all to what we were in that moment: human beings…nothing more or less… gathered to have brunch together and enjoy a football game. My dad stayed in the moment, cleaned up the mess, and something quippy, like, "Well, I didn't want that anyway," all helped me see it. *Stay in the moment and be human.*

Social phobia...what is that? Watching this all unfold and how my father dealt with the potentially catastrophic consequences of a flimsy paper plate finally giving way, perhaps at the worst possible moment, under the weight of my father's food, at what was easily the social event of the season cured—and I mean that word to its fullest definition—what I had been living with since I was a child: genuine social phobia.

The crippling social anxiety that had run my life since being a child was gone ...(snap of a finger)...just like that.

One-Liner: When you least expect it, and you choose your role models carefully, and you are fully present and paying attention, you never know when a moment will happen at the exact right time to cure what ails you.

Part II: Always bring a pen...

...As I alluded to in the above story, my father was a fairly well-known litigator in the Midwest, or at least in Ohio. Once we finally made it to the Ohio State stadium, affectionately known as "The Horseshoe" due to its shape, we took the only elevator that travels to such lofty heights and settled into our box seats. (Despite his drinking and choices of women, except for my mother, of course, I will not disparage my father; may he rest in peace. Not now. Not ever.)

We had just arrived in our seats, and being one of maybe two people wanting to actually watch the game, I sat, fixated on the beautiful field, the color of the scarlet and gray uniforms looking for my favorite players, when my dad informed me that he was going to walk around the suite, to see "what's what" and get something to drink. I told him that would be fine, and I was going to stay there, mesmerized. I chatted with a woman sitting next to me who was the second person interested in the game. About ten minutes later, my dad returned, drink in hand, and sat next to me. "Pssst, Beth-Anne, do you know who's here? Who is sitting right over there?" my dad asked me.

"No, Dad. Who?"

He looked around to make sure no one was watching him before he answered so as not to appear starstruck. "*Archie Griffin*!!" I must have had a look of confusion, even though I knew who he was, on my face because he continued, "The only man to win back-to-back Heisman trophies in college football."

"Where?" I replied.

"Over by the buffet," he said and jutted his chin in that direction.

"Oh, yeah! I see him!" I paused, thought about it for a second, and asked, "Will you go get his autograph?"

"You go get it!" he retorted.

"No, Dad, really, will you?"

"What do you want him to sign?"

I happened to have my Ohio State ball cap with me, maybe even wearing it; I can't remember. But I made a split-second decision. I took my hat off and handed it to my father. "Here! Have him sign it to Beth-Anne if you can!" We must have looked like two little kids who had just seen LeBron James.

Finally, my dad begrudgingly agreed. "You owe me!" he said, walking away, my ball cap in his hand. I waited. About ten minutes went by, and my dad came back, ball cap in hand. He had a blank stare on his face. "He doesn't have a pen." We both stared at each other. I searched my bag.

"I don't have one!"

He searched his pockets. "I don't either. Shit!" my dad mumbled.

Suddenly, the woman sitting next to me said, "I have one." It wasn't large enough to be a Sharpie, but it was black and fine-pointed. It would do the job.

"I don't want to go back to him again," my dad said. "This is so embarrassing!"

"Oh, come on!" I said, pleading.

Taking the pen from the woman, he said, "Oh, he is going to be so mad!"

"Dad, if it were either of us, we would be understanding!" My dad sighed.

"Okay, hurry, hurry, before he leaves," I said.

I am now the proud owner of an Ohio State ball cap with an autograph from the only man to win two Heisman trophies in a row in college football in 1974 and 1975: Archie Griffin.

One Liner: Always bring a pen and never underestimate the kindness of strangers 'cause you never know into whom you just might run.

Part III: Press Box introduction...

...Same day. You know, I think it is human nature to wonder if your parents are proud of you after they pass. I know my dad was proud of me. There toward the middle and end of his life, he would tell me. Of course, he would make fun of my profession and refer to me as a "shrink" all the time. Sure, we had some laughs. But this day was one of my prouder moments of my dad. I'm not sure that *I* ever got to tell him that.

Anyway, back to the game. My dad couldn't care less about the game. He was enjoying the "light fare" the lovely ABOTA folks had supplied us on this beautiful Saturday afternoon. Pulling himself away from all the conversations, my dad called me over to introduce me to some people in the next box. I reluctantly pulled myself away from the game and followed him. He introduced me to one of Ohio's Supreme Court Justices. Forgive me; her name escapes me right now. She was standing and chatting with the Governor of Ohio. Lo and behold, we were standing in the Governor's box. She, the Justice, looked at me and said, "Your father is the best trial attorney in the state of Ohio." And that is exactly how she introduced him to Governor Bob Taft. "The best trial attorney in the state of Ohio." I think he was as shocked as I was. That was probably a daughter's proudest moment: to hear your father introduced like that to some pretty important people.

Who knew that a day that started disastrously would wind up with a ball cap signed by one of the greatest Ohio State football players to ever play the game and hearing your father introduced to the Governor of the great state of Ohio as "the best trial attorney in the state"? I sure didn't.

One-Liner: In one day, I learned the cure to my own crippling social phobia, got some pretty cool sports memorabilia, and also had a pretty cool run-in with the governor; the words that got us there: humility, grace, and gratitude.

{ 32 }

Safe Versus Unsafe people: A Lesson From Snoopy…

…I am my own best friend. I don't know how to be a friend and not lead with empathy. Empathy leads someone else to talk. Someone else talking leads me to be quiet. And suddenly, the friendship is one-sided, and I'm exhausted. I believe I get enough stimulation just from the family I live with…my husband, my dog, and my parents-in-law. I cannot give anymore. This is why I have no friends.

We've been living here since 2019, almost exactly to the actual date I am writing this, and I have exactly zero friends. I don't get together with anyone. No one calls me to check on me. Not really, even my own family. Maybe I don't make a good friend. I will say that it is hard to be friends with anyone who needs me, as I am all tapped out of sympathy by the time I'm done working. Maybe that's the problem.

The introvert in me doesn't allow me to socialize with the other women I work with. They socialize over lunch every Wednesday. I do not like the smells of others' lunches; the laughter is loud; and worst of all, joining them would require for me to eat in front of others, a hallmark sign of social phobia: not being able to eat in front of others.

Boundaries. I respect them. Especially with people that I have deemed "unsafe" as opposed to "safe" in my life. If I don't have designated alone time, I am a bad human being to be around. I see too many clients to be emotionally available for others. Sometimes, I must say to my husband as he's talking about his day, "Sweet pea (that's what I call him), I am not hearing you right now. I can't." It is as if my brain must rest. And my husband is a "safe" person.

He will then recognize my needs and apologize. This is what "safe" people do. Safe people are those whom you trust. And not just in a way that trust implies, but rather you trust them not to use personal information you have shared with them against you. An unsafe person cannot be trusted with your secrets. It only takes one time for a person to go from being safe to unsafe. As a child, I learned very quickly who are safe and who are unsafe people.

People who are dishonest: unsafe. Throw you under a bus to save themselves: unsafe. People who care about you enough that they sacrifice themselves for you: safe. People who show up for you repeatedly: safe. Someone you can trust with your secrets or personal information: safe. As a shy, introverted young person, it is out of necessity that you are able to put people in one of those two categories.

Typically, once someone is in the unsafe bucket, it is very unlikely that they will suddenly become safe. And vice versa. Trust your gut and intuition. Unsafe doesn't mean bad; it just means they are bad for you; they are not healthy for you. The faster one learns how to do this, the less chance one stands of being hurt and repeatedly disappointed by unsafe people – because you simply expect less out of them. You do not expect them to protect you or even speak up for you. They hurt you and are not sorry. Please keep this in mind while you are building a social circle. The younger you are, the better. It does save some heartbreak.

I was a research assistant in my undergraduate years. I spent many afternoons in the attic of one of the academic buildings, without air conditioning, running experiments. Hanging on the wall of that small laboratory was a Snoopy poster. Snoopy was dancing his own little dance all by himself. The caption read, "Be your own best friend." Snoopy got it. I think true introverts will get it. If Snoopy gets it, I think the world stands a chance.

Making friends at work may not be safe. Being your own best friend, you will always be safe.

One-Liner: My personality is prohibitive to having friends. My job is prohibitive to having friends. I feel like my life is full enough for me. I have been a best friend to others. I have thought many people in my life were safe. Until I found out the hard way that they were not. When you are able to figure out who is unsafe and recognize that your needs and expectations will likely never be met by this person, it spares you from being let down when unsafe people do unsafe things to you. This is a skill I recommend you develop early in your life. We have to be so careful about who we let into our weird, quirky little worlds. Please choose carefully. I think Snoopy would be proud.

{ 33 }

Poodle Instructions or Paisley's Vocabulary...

...while my husband and I were gone for a week, I hired a dog walker/sitter for Paisley. She came to the house three times a day to walk and feed her. A cool grand I paid her for the week. Ridiculous? Maybe. To ensure the health and safety of the one I love? Absolutely worth it.

I decided it was best that I leave the dog walker instructions. There were tables, lists, and definitions on the page, snuggled amongst prose in the smallest font possible, and extended margins so that it would all fit onto one page. (Hoping that one page of instructions concealed the fact that I actually am one of them: an over-controlling, out in left-field, crazy pet owner).

Instead of including the tables, lists, and fonts for you here, I will attempt to put it all in prose (well, maybe not all of it...). What I would like to draw your attention to, first, is the section labeled: PAISLEY'S WORDS.

Now, for those of you who know a thing or two about Standard Poodles, this will make sense to you. I believe the breed currently ranks number two among the "who's who" of intelligent dogs. In short...they get it when you talk to them. Paisley gets it. So much so that I felt it was appropriate that our dog walker knows Paisley's vocabulary. It is lengthy. Some might say extensive, even for a person, let alone a dog. I felt it was important that the dog-walker be able to use words Paisley knows when talking to her, no matter what sort of distress Paisley might be in; I thought it important for anyone interacting with Paisley to use words she knew. Let's face it. It all comes back to mental health, both that of Paisley and whoever is interacting with her. It doesn't matter if the humans understand it as long as Paisley gets it.

Included on the list, in no particular order, were words like the following. Of course, we have "little potty" (or "LP") and "big potty" (or "BP"), so Paisley knows what to do when doing her business. If she gets in trouble or does something bad, she gets a "no, ma'am" or the dreaded "mama gonna spank-a-bottom." When she goes out to play, we spell P-A-R-K or B-A-L-L. She may be onto those by now, but we still spell them.

I've had only one other poodle who would get this on their list, but when Paisley wants a fresh drink, she will put her front paws on the counter in the kitchen or the bathroom. Normally, this is forbidden behavior, but when she does it, it means that she would like to take a drink directly from the faucet or have her bowl filled with fresh tap water. She is trying to tell you what she wants by putting her front paws on the counter. A fresh drink is what she wants. When we lived in Florida, this happened quite a bit, as you might imagine! When she did this, she was no threat to the food on the counter; she just needed water straight from the faucet.

Next, we have the obligatory "what to do in case of emergency." These included names and numbers of her local veterinarian and the local emergency pet clinic. Also included in these emergency numbers would normally be my mother and stepfather, several states away, because they know the decisions I would make if Paisley had a true emergency. However, on this particular trip, since all of my family would be with me and I had no idea what cell service existed in the middle of the ocean, the emergency numbers were limited to the professionals. The staff there know her best, know me pretty well, and speak her language as well as anyone.

The second to last important piece of information is MEDICINE. Paisley would do just about anything for a piece of cheese—you know, the single-sliced and wrapped American cheese. She swallows them practically whole and doesn't even notice a pill jammed into one. She knows the word "cheese," and her world stops when she hears it. So, all unpleasant things must somehow be incorporated into those 4" by 4" slabs of American cheese.

Last on the list was a note of caution: coyotes. We recently moved into a development in which all the houses back up to a forest. And with forests come creatures that call your backyard home. The most dangerous of all? Coyotes, who had been known to make meals out of small dogs. My limited understanding is that they are out mostly around dawn and dusk. Paisley was never off-leash, according to the rest of the manifesto; nevertheless, I felt as though the dog-sitter must be made aware of this new, unexpected-unless-you-are-looking-for-them, suburban threat to dogs.

That about summarizes Paisley's Instructions. Minus a few things, I think you get the gist.

One-Liner: The obvious one is telling all of the world to own a Standard Poodle at some point in their lives (e.g., see Travels with Charlie by John Steinbeck, 1962). The other One-Liner is: No matter who is in your life, at any moment, learn to speak "their language" so that they can understand *you, and most importantly, never leave them without letting them know how you feel about them in a way they can understand.*

{ 34 }

Stella and the Goose...

...As I mentioned, my husband, David, takes me to work every day. This started a while back when he wanted to make sure I got to work on time. (Didn't want me to get fired!) He's a musician, he's an architect, but most of all, and the majority of the reason I married him is that he has this wicked sense of humor. Not sharp; not aggressive (well, maybe sometimes); not wry (not even sure what that means); just goddamn funny!

Our car rides are often the only time in a day that we have together, as we are both very busy, and by the time we go to bed, we are too tired to talk; we eat dinner with family, so the conversation is only surface-level. On weekends, I end up sleeping in; he brings me Starbucks! So, our car rides together have become somewhat sacred. If we are fighting, we don't talk at all. If we argue, it's usually in the car. Here is one recent story from one of our car rides that brought a tear of laughter to my eyes.

Stella and the Goose
...a few years ago, I was living at a less-than-ideal apartment complex, as I had to move because my neighbor, who was also my landlord, asked me to go to dinner with him. I said no thank you, and things went downhill from there. I'm pretty sure he was a heavy user of something. Suffice it to say, he became paranoid and started

thinking I was spying on him, left a couple of threatening voicemails for me, and I ended up moving very quickly to a sublet in a huge apartment complex that was available, but not ideal, just to get away from him.

The new complex had multiple ponds on the property and, therefore, multiple waterfowl. A particularly unattractive goose had taken a liking to our little corner of heaven and every morning was outside our apartment door. I had two Standard Poodles at the time, Macy and Stella. Stella, I had raised since she was a puppy; I had adopted Macy from two gay men who "put her out to pasture" when they realized she was a small standard and not suitable to breed. Macy didn't like to exercise. Stella loved to run and was quite svelte.

Every morning, we'd come outside to go "little potty" or "LP," and she would see this particular goose. I say unattractive because he had an extra piece of skin that flopped over his beak and was a completely different color than his body. This was no mallard or Canadian goose, I'll say that much.

After Stella went LP, I would unhook her leash and let her chase the goose through the parking lot. She would chase him about fifty yards, just long enough for the goose to take flight and just far enough that she would come immediately back when the goose flew away. This didn't bother anyone in the complex, as it was early enough not many people were up, no cars moving about. I did not know David at that time in my life. In fact, we met that year while I was living in that complex.

Fast-forward in my life. Just a few months later, I met my husband-to-be, David. He went with me to test drive a new car. While I was test-driving the car, David and our new poodle, Paisley, came along. David walked Paisley around the grounds of the dealership while I bought a car. There must have been water somewhere, as there were Canadian geese wandering around the dealership. Paisley was in awe of the geese. As we were driving home from the dealership, he was telling me about Paisley and the geese, how much goose shit there was everywhere, and how our now new dog, Paisley, interacted with the geese.

Back to my memory of Stella, who would often catch up to the goose just before it took flight, but she would never try to catch it, capture it, bite at it, or anything. She would let it fly away, and then she'd run back to me. I remembered it fondly, as I miss all of my dogs who have passed. That day in the car, my husband sighed and said, "Ah, Stella and the goose. Sounds like the name of a short story, or a song, or the name of a band." He did know. He just didn't know us while we were living there, and this ritual was happening.

Stella died an early death—much before her time. In her memory, we did name my husband's parent's pontoon boat "The Stella Blue," after her, as she loved riding on that boat on Melrose bay. I do hope that somewhere in north central Florida, there is a boat floating around named The Stella Blue, giving some other family fond memories, like the ones I have of my dogs (Stella, Macy, and Safina) riding around on it for hours.

One of my other Standard Poodles, Macy, on the other hand, lived a long life and survived three other dogs in my life. I could tell many stories about Macy. She had seizures and congestive heart failure for the last three to four years of her life, lived well past what the veterinarians anticipated, and almost died on the off-roads of Kentucky after she overdosed on my stepdad's powdered yet caffeinated diet supplement. I remember seeing an emergency vet in some small town and getting them to flush out her system with fluids. For some reason, they then sent me home with fluids to continue to flush out her system once I got home. Her little heart was just beating a mile a minute. Once we returned to Gainesville, there she was, lying on our bed with an IV bag of fluids (thanks to me learning how to insert a subcutaneous IV into a dog) hanging precariously above her!

One of Macy's other quirks was her ability to go big potty literally anywhere—didn't matter—on David's boat, on a tennis court, on the dock, in the street...not really in the house, which was good, but she was not modest or shy. In fact, one day, Google Earth passed by and was taking photos of the house David and I were living in. They photographed the house just as David was bending over to pick up her big potty (BP) in the front yard. He had Macy's leash in one hand and her biodegradable bag of shit in the other. That Google-Earth photo was out in the world for years, and we laughed about it until it was finally changed!

Stella had her goose; Macy had David; Safina had her tennis ball and her ability to somehow always end up in the water despite not really knowing how to swim; Zoe would only drink fresh water directly from the faucet; and now Paisley, the little mouse in the house, has more love and affection than anyone in the house.

As a final aside, dogs are the living embodiment of what it means to be "present." They are happy when they see you; they are happy to get food, treats, walks, runs in the park, attention. I read once that just staring into your dog's eyes releases a hormone called "oxytocin," which is the "bonding" hormone in humans. Typically (though not always), they don't carry a grudge or keep an emotional "bank account" as we humans do; they don't talk back to us, and they rarely get mad at us; they aren't regretting yesterday or fretting about tomorrow (typically). They are alert and attentive in most every second they are awake. My mom tells the joke that goes something like, "So a man accidentally locks his ex-wife and his dog in the trunk of his car...who do you think is happy to see him when he finally gets it open?" The dog, of course, as the ex-wife is mad as hell. All I can say is please, please spend time around dogs. We can learn how to be present, in the truest sense of the word.

One-Liner: Related to Stella and her goose: more intelligent dogs may play different games than other dogs. Because Standard Poodles are so smart, they may find fun in strange things. And just like regular dogs, they can be a bit demanding of your attention. Therefore, I have, out of necessity, learned how to play what I call "the ignore game": no eye contact, no touching, no attending to, no rewards at all...simply ignore your demanding dog – or your husband. You get the idea.

{ 35 }

The Sign of the Signs...

...I am not sure I believe in signs. I'm not sure if I believe in the adage, "If it was meant to be, it will be." What I have realized, especially as I get older, is that I am open to the idea of signs. I had someone tell me the other day that when she was on public transport many years ago, she saw a sign on the bus advertising LEARN HOW TO SNOWBOARD. It was an advertisement for a resort in the Northeast where one could vacation and take snowboarding lessons. At the time, she was between jobs and may have even been on her way to a job interview, but there was something about that sign that piqued her curiosity. "I have always wanted to learn how to snowboard," she thought. Long story short, she went to the resort, learned how to snowboard, became a professional snowboarder, and eventually joined the resort to become an instructor. Talk about signs. Literally and figuratively.

Now, I am aware that this is perhaps an extreme example, but her example is well-taken. If we pay attention to our surroundings, sure, there are signs everywhere. I do mean that, literally and figuratively. For example, I can be in a random pharmacy chain store, and the exact song that inspired me to write my very first screenplay twenty years ago begins playing on the overhead PA system. Is that a coincidence or a reminder that I should not abandon what comes so naturally to my soul—writing? I don't know. I'll never know. Despite my limited success as a writer, I cannot *not* write. I could walk away from psychology tomorrow. I could not live without writing. Sitting down to watch television and seeing that the movie *A Few Good Men* is on, tuning to it at the exact part when Jack Nicholson says the line that I used in a play that I am writing...coincidence or a sign that I shouldn't stop writing? I don't know. I'll never know. But our interpretation of what things mean might be the critical piece here. If I choose to interpret that occurrence as a "sign" that I should not stop writing, maybe I will see the day that one of my plays, books, or screenplays actually touches someone someday.

One-Liner: Never stop paying attention; interpret things as you may but never stop being open to what the universe might be trying to tell you.

{ 36 }

I Want Versus I Need...

...I was wide awake in the middle of the night. I think of this often, but for some reason, I had a moment (or two) to really think about it: do I need it or just want it (whatever "it" is)? This is something that is frequently visited in what I now like to call "screenplay school." This refers to 2010 when I enrolled in a remote MFA program in screenplay writing. I did not graduate, though I had done all but my thesis. I could not tolerate being late in my life and having to behave like I was twenty years old.

Nonetheless, one of the things they talked about in screenplay school is when "constructing your characters" and, in particular, their "arc" in the film, understand that it is often the case that you give a character (as a writer) what they *need*, not what they *want*. Then, I was in session with a patient, and it occurred to me that this particular patient, if he really wanted change, needed to focus on what he needed, not what he wanted.

The reason this occurred to me in the middle of the night was because I was in so much pain I prayed. I can count on one hand the number of times I have prayed to a specific deity in my life. In that moment, I said, "God, please give me what I need, not what I want." Whatever that was, I was willing to risk it. Sure enough, my medication became available to me that day (or really the next day, as they had to special order it). Now, to me, this means I am not addicted to it, but my body truly needs it to settle down when I am experiencing so much pain. Sure enough, I only had to miss one day of work. I got what I needed, which was relief from my pain.

This question is much deeper than I am describing here. When you work with people as intimately as I do, sometimes the conversation goes something like, "I want to meet someone, fall in love, and have kids." As a therapist, I'm thinking, and likely saying, what they need is a group, a family, a tribe to belong to. What they need to do is to love themselves wholly and completely, so if this never happens for them, they will feel good about who they are as human beings, find their "people," and put themselves in situations to meet other grounded, like-minded people who could become potential partners.

If I have a surgeon as a patient who is highly respected in her field but feels disconnected from her family, it is my job as a psychologist to figure out what she needs, not what she wants. She *wants* to be close to her family (a wife and two children, in this case) when maybe what she really needs is to deal with emotions from her childhood. I asked her, "Tell me what it was like when your father abandoned you, your mother, and your sister when you were ten years old." And, of course, she is wondering what that has to do with why she cannot connect with her own family because she wants a better "work-life balance."

What she needed was to connect with those twenty-year-old issues of abandonment. She wanted to work on her sleep hygiene and to better manage her time, thinking this was the key to connecting with her current family. What she needed was something entirely different. Revisiting those emotional wounds and having peace with them was the best way, in my opinion, to reconnect with the family she had created.

It is a therapist's job to take you on a journey that you need, rather than just give you what you want, or are asking for, which is usually just based on our egocentric, delayed reinforcement, impulsivity, give me "the tools" now, Gen Z-type thinking.

A good shrink (admittedly hard to find) will lead you on a seemingly circuitous route to where you want to get rather than take you directly there and only there. If you want to go through a forest, the easiest way is from point A to B. The more difficult, challenging, and annoying route will get you to the same point B, only your knees will be scraped and bruised, your hair will be filthy, and your clothes tattered, but *that*, to me, is the more "corrective" journey—and you will learn a whole lot more about your life, than if the shrink had gotten a golf cart and a machete and driven you directly to point B, teaching you a few survival skills along the way.

I'm not saying God gave me my medicine. I'm saying we wish for things we want, not what we need, which is usually something that is healthy and good for us in a way that doesn't entirely make sense at the time.

One-Liner: Take a minute, any minute, and hope that your life gives you what you need, not just what you want; you'll thank me for it, I promise. Even better...ask the Universe to give you what you need...not what you want.

{ 37 }

Blessings in Disguise...

..."Blessings" is a word I rarely use. I'm not sure why. Could be I am much more spiritual than religious, and I believe that word is reserved for those truly dedicated to God, a source of the blessings we receive. Nonetheless, I am going to use it here, one of the times I felt truly blessed.

The year was 2010, back when I did have friends, and I had taken advantage of the Family Medical Leave Act (FMLA) of 1993. I had been verbally assaulted by the director of the counseling center at one of the universities at which I was working. It happened in my office, with a colleague of mine in the room, who, by the way, had consoled me at the time it happened, then later "couldn't remember" exactly what had happened.

Jackie, an African American male, was the director of my contingent in this "hostile takeover," which was actually just the merging of two mental health facilities at the university for whom I was working and the man who had hired me. He was not selected to run the "new" counseling center. Rather, they brought in someone from the outside to take the helm. The new director-wanted to meet with me and a colleague of mine, as we oversaw a program that was an important part of our "sides." She was verbally abusive to me.

Long story short, I resigned from my position. The new director was terminated a few years later, but not for being unkind to people, ironically. I think she was terminated because of misappropriation of funds. During her time as a director, there were multiple complaints about her. Some people left; some retired; some got abused and stayed under her leadership.

Often, we think, "They could never be without me...etc." Right? Wrong. We are all disposable in our jobs. As important as I thought I was in that position, it turns out I wasn't important at all. Despite the outpouring of support I got, I left the university after eight years of dedicated service. That's the short version of the story.

Two years after the hostile takeover, Roberta (may she rest in peace) decided to host a reunion of our contingency just to check in to see each other again. All the clinicians and administrators who made up our tight little group gathered at Roberta's house to reminisce, recollect, and share times like we used to. Jackie was there. I went by myself, worried I might be shunned for leaving the way I did, but not only was I welcomed with open arms, but I was almost celebrated for having left.

As I looked around the room at my former coworkers, it left Jackie and me dumbfounded. Our previously happy, connected, and collected colleagues looked like veterans who had been through a war. They were all walking around with some sort of alcoholic beverage in their hands. They were expressionless, a bit haggard, and aged at least ten years, though it had only been two. I walked into a war-torn crowd, but there were no bruises or blood. What I found was twenty-five human beings who were barely conscious, wandering around; hair grayer...skin pallid...outfits monochromatic. The young, healthy, and vibrant group of which I was once part had been suffering under the tyrannical reign. Each had a story of being yelled at, punished, or shamed at her hands, but instead of leaving, even in the unfortunate way I did, they stayed. They had endured. They had barely survived.

Of the people there, I think Jackie and I were the only ones who had managed to escape. He was now running the Employee Assistance Program (EAP) for the University of Florida (which I would join soon). I was in private practice and had become an adjunct professor at a neighboring community college.

I remember all of us sitting in a circle. I shared stolen glances with Jackie as if to say, "What has happened to these people?" They were trying not to compare war stories, but those came out anyway. People were trying to be supportive and share the good times we had had when we were last together, only for their stories to be overshadowed by grief. Sadness for what was, sadness for losing the camaraderie, for losing Jackie, and the overarching sadness of losing the battle, the "hostile takeover." Seeing those who you had once shared a battlefield with now having their souls excised from their bodies was heartbreaking.

In a spare moment, Jackie and I passed by each other. He whispered to me, "Blessings come in all disguises, you know, Beth-Anne." Understanding completely and wholly what he was saying to me, I quietly whispered, "I can see that now, Jackie."

One-Liner: The Universe gave me what I needed: sense enough to get the hell out of there, but in a very painful and scary way. To stay would have been catastrophic for me. Blessings come in all disguises. Amen.

P.S. I don't think one should ever think that they are "one of a kind" or not disposable at their jobs. They'll be just fine without you. I'm sorry...I think that is true for 99% of working folk, no matter how high you think you are to people.

{ 38 }

When to Quit a Job...

...I don't know if you have heard this expression, but I have, and I think it deserves a mention. It goes something like, "You don't leave jobs; you leave people." Some examples are employees who want to leave their jobs, are typically unhappy in their current position, are in a "bad-fit" situation, or are typically unhappy with how they are being treated by their coworkers or management. This is something I have worked with consistently now for ten-plus years. "When and what is it going to take for me to leave this job?"

I can't answer that question for anyone else. What I will do is help someone understand what a toxic work environment is, what a work-life balance is, what action they are being called to do, is this job is doing that, and the difference between a job, a career, and a calling. These are questions I will happily discuss and process. The one question I will surely ask is, do you like the people you are working with and for? If you are ever lucky enough to have a boss like Jackie, as I did for thirteen years, I'd say you struck gold. If money is the name of the game, then I might not be preaching to the right choir. If you have a boss who cares about you, and your colleagues are genuine and are people who, no matter what, have your back because they honestly believe in you, you may be the richest of us all. And if you are contemplating leaving said job, I would say, please tread carefully and thoughtfully. In my experience, there is no better job than having colleagues and a boss who gives you all of that because they have vetted you, first, out of all their applicants, and second, hired you because they believe in your ability to do for the job, then gold it is.

Case in point...if you had asked me when I was younger, in my teens, even in college or in graduate school, if I would ever live in Florida, my answer would have been a loud and resounding, "Hell, no!" As it happened, the first job I was offered out of graduate school (after I had completed my pre-doctoral internship in Laramie, Wyoming, and my post-doctoral training in a small town in Ohio) was in Florida. At the time, my dad's sister and her husband and daughter lived in Florida. Their daughter, my cousin, was the director of the pharmacy at the Student Health Care Center, and it turned out that the mental health team at the SHCC needed a psychologist. The salary was quite low. But I flew down, interviewed, and after spending the day with those who would become my future colleagues, I could not have said no. I knew at the interview that I was moving to Florida if offered the job.

The actual story is that right after my interview in Florida and return to Ohio, I left for California for a friend's wedding. In a parking garage at LAX, sitting in my rental car, my phone had so many missed calls and messages; the "one and only" Jackie was "looking for me." He couldn't find me because I was flying across the country during a time when you had to turn off all cellular devices while in flight. The salary was low (sorry, Jackie). But the benefits alone were worth $30,000. For someone who does not tolerate the heat well and had just closed on a condominium in Ohio—the one and only time I have owned property—the job was too good to pass up. To Florida I went. Fifteen years later, Jackie retired; my job was outsourced; I had to jump on the job market for the first time in a long time; that train took me to Durham, North Carolina.

Gainesville was the right place for me at the right time. I like to say that I "grew up there, professionally." My memories of Gainesville will always be fond ones. I met and married my husband there. I got to be with my aunt, uncle, and cousin again.

My uncle ended up passing away from a cruel cancer at a devastatingly young age. Remember, you have to take the good with the bad, if you are living in an honestly present way. But I got to know them while they were still in the prime of their lives. I got to know a part of the "Blue" side of my family (i.e., my father's side, because our last name is Blue) who I wouldn't have otherwise. My husband and I had a beautiful wedding at the Herlong Mansion in Micanopy, Florida, which was perfect (as everyone thinks theirs is…but really ours was. All in all, they were some of the best years of my life. I wouldn't trade them for anything, not because I miss Florida and the goddamn heat, but because I miss Jackie and my precious colleagues I had the privilege of working with and knowing there.

One-Liner: People leave people, not jobs. To me, there is little better than being valued by those around you: feeling genuinely supported by people who care about your well-being, trust you, and support you unconditionally, even if you make a huge mistake. If you do decide to leave a place of employment, please do yourself a favor and consider who, not what, you are leaving. And then consider them again, for me…and for yourself.

{ 39 }

Be Purposeful...

...while I have you, while you are paying attention, and while you are actively participating in a journey like no other—a shrink shrinking herself—I believe this chapter is relevant to psychologists, writers, and everybody in between.

Let's just take psychologists and writers, for example, since I am both. I might even go as far as saying that for any "artist," and I use that term as liberally as I possibly can, everything they do, say, and write in the production of any work of art is deliberate; it is specific, and it serves a purpose.

Therapy, for example, I consider an art form. People don't realize that, especially my patients or colleagues. Anything I do while practicing psychology is on purpose. But for the sake of argument, I'm going to use a therapy session as our jumping-off space. If I am doing my job, am present, and paying attention at every level, as I should be doing... everything I do, say, or maybe omit is on purpose. Let me say that again. If I am completely present and paying attention, which are the underlying notions of this entire book, everything is on purpose. Whether I am shaking your hand, giving you a box of tissues, or taking a sip of my coffee, and those don't even have anything to do with the therapy itself, is being done on purpose and for a specific reason. If I lean forward in my chair, it means something. If I put my feet up on my coffee table, it means something. Every arrangement in my office, every tear that I shed (no, it is not uncommon for me to cry with my clients), every time I do not talk if I adjust my glasses, it is on purpose. I don't know if all clinicians are like this. I think that if a therapist has been trained well and was, and still is, paying attention, then they at least have a shot at doing a good job. If you follow when I say I am able to easily leave my work at work and come home to be 100% with my family when it is time, you understand that it is much easier to do if I am present and purposeful while working with a client.

I'll switch to writing now. Every letter, every punctuative symbol, every sentence structure is purposeful...exactly the way I want it to be. It expresses the exact way I am feeling, allowing me to communicate exactly what I am trying to communicate. There are no "mistakes" or "coincidences" in either writing or therapy. It goes the way it goes, and it reads the way it reads because I want it to. I don't think I have a unique or even complete understanding of the rules of grammar or even of the human language. I do, however, know exactly what it is that I want to say or communicate at almost every moment.

There are two compliments I've received over the years from clients who have stuck with me. The first is to the above point. I was supervising a psychiatric resident and talking about my use of words and actions while in a session with a client. She looked at me and said, "You are surgical with your words..." which I took to mean I was precise, specific, and said exactly what I meant, and meant exactly what I said. I was trying to teach her the same.

The second compliment came from a man I was seeing while he was an undergraduate student. I was extremely late, back in the day, to everything, including my clients' appointments. He had waited maybe half an hour to see me. I apologized for being so late, which had already been established as a pattern for us. And he said, "You know what, Dr. Blue? When I come to see you, it's like going to a nice restaurant. Even if you must wait an hour, the food makes it entirely worth it."

Maybe those don't seem like great compliments to you, but to me, they meant the world. I have carried them with me all these years. I wanted to share them with you, at least the former, because she is exactly right, or at least what I aim to be: surgical with my words in therapy.

Then I digress. Back to writing...every period, pause, or reflection at just the right moment is critical. If I'm batting one thousand, I will leave "shrinking" or writing exactly where I wanted to so I can be present for whatever is next in my day. Nothing that happens in therapy is accidental. I say what I mean and mean what I say. I hand you a tissue to model what self-care looks like. If I tell a client, "I am right here," that usually means that I need them to feel safe or lower their voice. It's all part of the same equation. It is crafted and purposeful. Do I get it wrong? Of course. Do I screw up? Absolutely, and hopefully, with minimal damage to those in the room with me. Flexibility and adaptability (especially if you have got something wrong) are also critical. That's why it is an art form. How can you recognize if you got it wrong or screwed something up? Be present enough to hear and respond to the criticism, and everyone will tell you, in some kind of way, that you've done something right or wrong. Your job then is to listen to it, change it, clarify it, or just be humble enough to admit your mistake.

Back to the writing of screenplays: every line, every punctuation, every word is there for a reason; it serves a purpose and certainly didn't just "happen" to be there. It's there for a reason and sometimes it's a reason only the artist understands.

Lastly, on this topic, I've said it before, and I'll say it again: being present one hundred percent of the time with a client or when I write is my gift to you. How many friends will listen to you without multitasking or being distracted by something else? Likely, not many. We all have things going on in our lives, which is why therapy is different from talking to a friend. If you are my client, you have one hundred percent of my attention one hundred percent of the time I am with you. And if I do that correctly, I have no regrets about my day; I go home with little on my mind because I gave it "my all" in every moment. Even if that means I run over my "therapeutic hour" with a client because I need to finish the session right, I will do that. I would do that for any of my clients. If I run overtime, there is a good reason. Again, purposeful, present, and precise—in all that you do, especially with your time, your speech, and your art...that is the goal.

One-Liner: Be present and be purposeful in all that you do. Speak, write, act with purpose: it will free you to enjoy all of your day.

{ 40 }

Bollards, Scuppers, and Downspouts, Oh My…

...these are three words I have gone through my entire life without knowing and seemed to have gotten along just fine. Architectural, they are.

Apparently, bollards are cylindrical, large "pipes" coming up from the ground, full of concrete to tell you where you cannot drive. Or said another way, they are in places like banks or parking garages to guide vehicles through what is sometimes a labyrinth of a parking structure. They are full of cement, so if you hit them, 1) you'll know it, and 2) it will damage your car. Parking lots and restaurants with a drive-through often have them. They are not flexible, and they will not give if you run into one.

My understanding of a downspout and a scupper is a little hazy, but if I see them, I can now recognize them. And to think, my whole life! From what I can tell, these are conduits on the side of structures that allow rainwater, or otherwise pooled water, to drain downward. Makes sense. Water seems harmless enough, but *en masse* can be quite rageful and damaging. The downspouts and scuppers are there to make sure the damage from collected water is minimized.

As I think about how my husband explained these to me, it occurs to me that these might be helpful things to have in life. If we were guided through the "labyrinth" of life and choices by unforgiving "posts" that say—*not this way—nope, not there—stay in your "lane,"—I think* that would be quite helpful. And maybe a caution sign: IF YOU HIT THIS, BE PREPARED TO GET A DENTED PSYCHE or A FRACTURED HEART. At least you would know now that going a certain way or making a certain choice is only going to cause unproductive harm and damage. If we could avoid it, I'm quite certain we wouldn't hit that bollard again! And let's build in some scuppers and downspouts while we're at it.

If there is an excess of something that *en masse* could be disruptive, let's give it a release valve, a place to go. Dysfunctional family? "Down the scupper." Toxic relationship? "Safe trip through the downspout!" Either way, the excess that accumulates for potential mass destruction has a place to go: to be drained from our lives. If architects are so careful in designing these sorts of devices, perhaps we could learn a thing or two from them. Although, with all the bollards and downspouts, there may not be any allowance for veering off the path or suffering through a broken heart. And what fun would that be? Again, I went forty years without knowing these words...forty years!

One-Liner: If we had our paths chosen for us in life, or if we had a release valve to allow toxic things to pour down and away from us, life might be a little easier! Maybe having these will help us with navigation. Occasionally, we hit a bollard, or a downspout gets blocked and overflows, and we make a mistake in our life. That's okay. Next time we make the bollards stronger, taller, and sturdier...and we make the downspouts wider so more shit can go down them; that's how we, and architects, learn to create a plan that avoids mass casualties. I'm just saying it might be nice to have some of those boundaries already in place as we go through our lives.

{ 41 }

Setbacks and Pork Chops...

...speaking of architecture, a few years ago, my husband and I were considering adding an independent apartment above his parents' garage for us to live in. Plans were drawn up—in fact, multiple plans—meaning actual blueprints. Thought was put into things like a laundry room, stairs location, different points of access to the main house, county building codes, and "sweat equity" if we did some of the work ourselves. These were all discussed. For me, I got excited and emotionally invested.

A few days later, my husband sat me down, with plans in hand, looked at me, and said, or I heard something like, "Sweetie, there are some setbacks." *Oh, no!* I thought. Setbacks? What setbacks? What has gone wrong now? Seeing what I could only imagine was the look of disappointment on my face, he quickly replied, "No, not those kinds of setbacks!" Turns out, setbacks refer, architecturally, to the distance between the property line and where a building structure can be built. Again, for forty years of my life, I went without knowing the meaning of this term. "Oh, setbacks!" I replied. "Sure, how many feet are we looking at...?"

Pork chops were a meal we had frequently when I was a child. Well, forty years later, a new meaning to a culinary dish arises. Fast forward from the above story to the addition not getting built, likely due to actual *financial* setbacks. Ironically, my husband and I are driving around town one day, sometime later, looking at houses for sale. Aesthetically, I am clear on what I like and don't like. Remarkably, my husband and I share similar tastes. However, as we are driving around looking at houses just from the car, both new construction and old, he suddenly makes a comment akin to, "No, no, no! You would think architects know how to properly design a pork chop. I mean, look at that!" I'm already at my wit's end, having just been driven around all afternoon looking at houses, I have absolutely no idea what he is talking about, and at that moment, I must admit I am trying to decide if I even care! Apparently, a "pork chop" in architectural terms refers to where the "easement" (again, forty years...) meets the roof meets the external wall on a house—which in my mind looks like when there is a point (fulcrum) in a roof, say, around a window and the roof or easement (overhang) must rejoin with the outside of the house—and those points at which these things all converge—are called pork chops. They can be flushed with the outside wall; they can match the easement; they can be curved or come to a natural straight point, like the angles of a triangle, etc. Good grief! I think at that point, whether I feigned interest or not, my interest had waned, and my husband was off and running on a rant about pork chops and how it was done wrong on each and every house we looked at.

For the love of God, just take me home and make me a nice pork chop on a platter! How's that? Forty years, I tell you, forty years!

One-Liner: Architecture imitating life; maybe I like my pork chops well done. Apparently, and luckily, so does my husband!

{ 42 }

Maximizing Fun Factor...

...we were at a vacation beach home near the Atlantic Ocean as a family and could not get the TV to work. Oh, the horror! We might actually have to sit around and talk to each other. Oh, dear. Fear not, everyone brought their respective devices, and we did get Wi-Fi. But my husband decided we needed to watch *The Masters Golf Tournament*, as it was Sunday, the day the winner was crowned or adorned with *the* green jacket. So, to Wal-Mart he goes in search of a Roku to see if that will get us "Live at the Masters" on TV. An hour later, lo and behold, he returns with a device, plugs it into the TV, and now, the TV starts doing whatever it does to integrate the Roku so that we can see, as a family, if Tiger, in one of his many comebacks, proves himself as a professional golfer one more time.

As the television goes through its steps of setup, like "loading channels," a screen suddenly pops up that reads, "Maximizing Fun Factor." No, I don't know the good people at Roku, but, man, what a job that would be—developing a program that maximizes the "fun factor." At the same time, how do they know what fun is? Fun for one person might not be fun for another. And who are they to decide what fun means for my family or the Roku masses? Who's thinking of them? Maybe watching Tiger is not fun for everyone, even though, admittedly, we had purchased the Roku just so we wouldn't have to discuss what was meaningful in our lives, and at that moment, it was the Green Jacket. As an aside, we are all sports fans, all kinds of sports, all ages of fans. That is the one thing our families have in common, thank God! But there it was, right on the screen. Displayed prominently was the "percentage complete" number of the FUN FACTOR. It was slowly rising, just like the "loading channel" screen did. I wondered what was going to happen when it got to one hundred percent. Maybe the TV would explode. Maybe that was their idea of fun. Or "just kidding" would come on the screen, accompanied by the words, "SUCK IT! Or maybe a cartoon for children would pop up, or a game that is universally fun would begin. The mind reels with possibilities. Anyway, I doubt Roku really knows what fun they are maximizing…but I can tell you this. However, they maximized it; not only did it heighten my expectations, which perhaps might have been their only goal, but I decided I needed a device in my life to maximize my "fun factor" because, so far, that button has eluded me!

One-Liner: Damn those folks at Roku…where do they get off, thinking they know what my fun factor is, and how dare they even try to maximize it. I'll maximize your fun factor, and you can see how it feels. Such a tease…it was a good tournament, though…damn it! In actuality, we do not need some streaming device to have fun anyway. We're family. We love each other. And God help us if we have to have TV brought to us by Roku to have fun!

{ 43 }

Diversity and Inclusion…

…I work in higher education. First of all, I don't really know what that means, "higher education." I guess higher than high school? Sounds a bit elitist. I am a proponent of furthering one's education, but I'm not sure we need to put a value or label on it. One of the ideals on college campuses lately is "diversity and inclusion." This interests me because the words themselves when juxtaposed as they are, seem oxymoronic. Diversity seems to imply that we recognize and celebrate our differences. Inclusion is to include everyone in something no matter what they look like, from where they come, or the troubles they've had. I think the point is that underprivileged or disadvantaged groups need to have a presence or a voice.

To my point, I feel disadvantaged or disenfranchised. Mental illness runs in my family. I have diagnosable mental health disorders and have been treated for them. But I don't get put in a "disadvantaged group." So, who's looking out for me? I mean, which is it? Are we going to get behind the idea of including everyone no matter their group identity, or are we going to make sure that each diverse (read different) group has a voice that needs to be heard separately?

I've heard a different idea somewhat recently. I think it is true: as human beings, we have far more in common than we do differences, no matter what groups we include ourselves in. Let's celebrate that. Let's celebrate humanity. Humility. Let's level the playing field and give everyone an equal chance to succeed. I'm not sure we need a catchy slogan to do this. We all belong to the Human Race and therefore, we all deserve equality. Let's celebrate our commonalities, not try to diversify inclusively! Just the words next to each other... right?!

One-Liner: I've been accused of not knowing or recognizing my "white privilege." Here, again, is the irony. I recognize my white privilege every day. Do you know why? I am in the minority, even in my own family. I struggle with mental illness; I have a doctorate degree in clinical psychology. Maybe I did that to try to heal myself. I don't know. What I do know is I have had to work extra fucking hard to get where I am, given my disabilities. Do I treat all people equally? Yes. Have I been treated fairly my whole life? Absolutely not. Just because my skin is white, make no mistake, I am calloused; I am bruised; I have been broken multiple times in my life. To those who do not think I know what it is to struggle, I suggest putting them in a psychiatric facility for a week or two. My skin may not know what "privileged" means. But my heart and soul sure do. In fact, I believe that allows me to better understand other under-served communities. I am different, so include me.

{ 44 }

The Universe Is Never Wrong...

(This phrase was also considered as a title for this book as I do find it profound.)

...I share my birthday with a friend of mine since ours are only a couple of days apart. We have taken a couple of trips together in celebration over the years. The most recent, which included four women, was a difficult one for me. I was at the beginning of my rheumatologic illness and just a few months out from having lost both of my dogs. As is my nature, I decided to take a break from the group and spend a little time at the resort pool by myself. I was feeling bad about my body, as I had gained some weight because of the illness and treatment; I was feeling despondent over the loss of my dogs; just generally feeling discontent with where I was in my life.

I stayed in the pool for a while, despite my disgust at being in a bathing suit, and paddled around a bit. There was a smattering of other guests in and around the pool. I tend to be aware of others around me. I don't care to "people watch," as I don't want others watching me, so why would I spend time watching them? Ironically, this surprises people when I tell them this because of my profession as a psychologist. People always say to me, "Oh, you must love to watch and analyze people!" *I do it for a living, for heaven's sake! Why would I do it on my own time, too?*

I was minding my own business only to hear a man talking loudly on his phone. Never mind that he was disturbing the general serenity of the water, he was talking so loudly I could make out enough of what he was saying to figure that he had to have been some type of salesperson. I don't know if it was high-end real estate or vacuum cleaners he was selling, but suddenly he said to whom I can only assume was his client on the other end (hopefully not his wife!) the most intriguing words: "Well, the universe is never wrong!" Or perhaps he said it conversely, "The universe is always right." I repeated the sentiment in my head a few times and simply ended my internal dialog with a *Huh...that's an interesting way to look at the world*; in a similar way, I might respond to a devoutly religious person saying, "Well, it's as God intended." I must admit, though, that this happened several years ago, and here I am writing about it. The universe is never wrong. The universe is never wrong. The universe is never wrong.

Coincidentally, there is a random piece of art hanging in the bathroom where I worked, which was created by a client of my colleague (see Chapter 4), that has a similar line, "Trust the universe." I also must admit I like the word "universe" as opposed to "God" or some other type of deity. Just hits my ear better. But, if the universe is never wrong, then we are where we are in our lives for a reason. The people who are part of our lives are part of a reason. Are we in love and on top of the world for a reason? Or conversely, are we brokenhearted and jobless for a reason?

I don't know the answers to these questions, despite being asked them frequently, but can you imagine me giving the explanation of "This is how God intended it," to my clients in the depths of their despair? No. Nor do I give them explanations like "The universe is never wrong" or something as trite as "If it was meant to be, it will be" to my clients. I do think, however, that I like this expression, or at least it gives me pause.

For example, I finally decided to apply to rescue a dog the other day, my first expression of a desire to have a dog in my life since mine passed nearly three years ago. This dog was a senior of the breed I was looking for, her owner having recently passed away. This meant I wouldn't have the dog but for a few years, probably three or five at best given the breed. Some might say, why on earth would you get a dog only to have it die in a couple of years and go through that tragedy all over again? Some might say it could be nice to give an older dog a good home for however long it lives, hopefully bringing joy to my life for that time as well. I submitted my application; I talked to the daughter of the woman who had passed away who had the dog; I talked to my current landlord about having the dog. And I said to myself, you know what? I'm going to let the universe decide if this dog is mine to have. It did. I did not get the dog. I am okay with that.

I got married to my husband, and we got Paisley together a couple of years after that. There have been some bumps in the road, but we are living happily ever after.

One-Liner: Pay attention to everything going on around you. If I had been on my phone or listening to music, I would never have overheard some random salesperson say some random line to some random customer—and I would have missed a gem! Also, if there is something or someone out there making life decisions for us, then what the hell? I've agonized over decisions, and for what? I would like to think I have some say in my life. So, I am going to choose to believe that free will exists...even if someone or something else is pulling the strings.

{ 45 }

How We Got Paisley...

...my husband, bless his heart, had never been through a dog adoption before. I found a dog through Standard Poodle Rescue, and she was in Tarpon Springs, Florida, a couple of hours from our house; she was two years old and black. Just what we wanted. We had to drive to meet her to see if it was a good match. Apparently, there was another family interested in her. They already had a male "Standard" (Poodle), and the family whose house she was in was a little worried about Paisley being around a dominant male poodle. We thought that would work to our advantage.

It was August 27, 2017. It was a Sunday. We pulled up in front of this beautiful home in Tarpon Springs at the agreed-upon time. This home had a screened-in pool and lots of room, and the woman who "ran" the shelter had brought Paisley home with her. We walked in and met Paisley. I'm not going to say it was "love at first sight," but we were both taken with her. She was timid but warmed up to us quickly. After all, we were there to see what Paisley thought of us, not the other way around.

We interacted with Paisley in front of this woman. Paisley sat near both of us, leaned on us (she's still a leaner), play-chewed my engagement ring (poodles love hands), and played with David, too. All in all, it was a great visit. Better than great, it was like having a job interview and feeling so good about yourself and how it went when it was over. Then the woman turned to us and said something like, "Well, I'll have to see how she does with the other couple and their dog, then I'll call you tomorrow." What? You'll call us tomorrow? I could just feel my husband's anxiety slowly turning into anger. He said, "Well, we aren't leaving here. We'll spend the night up the road, and that way, after you choose us, we can come right back to get her." The woman said, "Okay," and we left without Paisley.

We get in the car, and my husband says, "What just happened? What was that?"

And I said, as gently as I could, "Sweet Pea, this is how it works when there is more than one person interested in the dog...they have to find the best fit for the dog."

To which he said, "I don't understand...why aren't we taking her home?" He was so devastated that we didn't have her.

I finally said, "You know what...we passed some outlet malls on the way here, just outside of town. Why don't we go there and just walk around for a bit."

"But I don't understand...we killed it! She loved us," he repeated.

"I know, but we are not the ones who decide."

"But she's our dog!"

"Come on...take me to J. Crew," I finally said.

And off we drove, heartbroken. I even used the "job interview" analogy with him, explaining that it is not up to us, as we drove.

"We don't choose; the lady does!" I explained sternly, trying to hide my broken heart as well.

"But I don't understand...she's perfect for us...We are perfect for her!"

"Please, just drive," I insisted.

We finally reached the outlet mall about a half hour later. He couldn't get out of the car. I don't think he was crying. He just kept repeating the same things about how we were perfect for her. I finally said, "You go park. I'm going to walk around for a while. I'll text you in about twenty minutes and let you know where I am."

I exited the vehicle as he was still mumbling about how perfect we were and that he couldn't believe what had just happened.

Somehow, I ended up at the Coach store. I was just wandering around, aimlessly. I finally sought out the jewelry display...I like a Coach bangle from time to time. There was one that caught my eye. It was Lucite or acrylic. It was a black bangle, with a pink floral pattern all the way around. It was quite lovely. A salesman approached me, noticing I was noticing the bangle.

"Can I help you?" he said. I started to explain to him that my husband was the one out in the parking lot, in the gray Toyota, and quite distraught...when I caught myself, and told him which *piece of jewelry* I was interested in. He politely retrieved it from the case, commenting—"It's been one of our biggest sellers this summer!" I slipped it on my wrist. Admiring it, he said something like, "Everything in the store is an additional ten percent off." I looked at it a few seconds longer and decided I needed what I call a "feel better" gift for myself.

Standing in line to buy the bracelet, my phone made a dinging sound. I figured it was my husband telling me to hurry up, as he often does when I'm shopping. I got my phone out of my bag and looked down at it. It was from a Tarpon Springs number, not a Gainesville number. It was a text. It was one line. "Paisley chose you." I quickly called the number, just beside myself with joy. I said, "Is it true? Did she really pick us?"

"Yes. I shouldn't have had let you leave," I heard the woman say on the other end of the phone.

"We're just up the road at the outlet mall. We can be there within the half-hour."

Of course, the line took forever. I couldn't text my husband because the service was so bad in the store, although I think I got one text to go…something like, "She chose us!"

I bought my bracelet, that I still have and wear to this day, ran out of the store, and to our car, where my husband was. He was still in the car, wondering what we had done wrong, having not received my text about what had happened, because of bad cell service. I opened the driver's side door, and yelled, "She chose us!"

"What?"

"The woman, Susan, she just texted! Paisley chose us!"

After a jumping hug around the car, we drove back to get our little "mouse," as I call her now. She changed our lives forever. She has lived in two houses with us in Gainesville; now, two houses with us in Durham. She's been flying with us in my stepdad's airplane;

we organize family reunions with my husband's family in only "dog-friendly" places; she has been in pools, hotels, countless houses, cars, and states in America. And she is the best little girl we could have asked for...and we have lived "happily ever after" ever since that fateful day in Tarpon Springs.

One-Liner: Don't count your chickens (dogs) before they hatch (belong to you) ...it can be devastating! And please, learn about the (adoption) process before one enters said process, so at least you know what to expect. Additionally, as my husband and I were driving down to meet Paisley, we must have come up with a dozen alternate names for her. But when we were turned away, knowing she belonged to us, and then knowing she chose us, we knew she was going to be our dog, Paisley.

{ 46 }

Speaking of Poodles...

And Overcoming Crippling Shyness...

...when I was in graduate school at Palo Alto University, I got my first dog as a gift. She was a black Standard Poodle, and my dad brought her when he met me at the airport as I flew home from Christmas one year. He surprised me with her by bringing her into the baggage claim area with a big red Christmas bow tied around her neck. I had picked her out when she was a baby, so I knew she was coming. My dad had her groomed; the memory of her bounding through the airport (this was pre-911) was priceless.

I decided to name her Zoë, which means "life" in some circles, whichever circles put an umlaut over a vowel, making it a "hard e." I got her when she was twelve months. Very early in her life, we went to obedience training. I won't forget this experience because everyone in the class loved her. Who wouldn't? She was just a pup, she was beautiful, prancing around, but, holy cow, was she naughty. She would grab the end of the toilet paper in the holder and just run around the apartment. She did the same thing with paper towels if she got hold of one end of the roll. She barked, she cried from her crate, she pulled me on the leash...just like a toddler, pushing all my boundaries.

I remember our first day of puppy obedience class; a gentleman raised his hand (we were without our dogs for the first class) and asked, in all seriousness, what kind of treats we were supposed to buy as reinforcement in the class. The instructors looked at each other, then back at him. "None," was the reply. The reinforcement we use in this class is love. I believe that is one of the Dog Whisperer's top three priorities: exercise, discipline, and love (I believe in that order)." We all looked at each other, and I knew we were all thinking, "Huh...okay...my love for my dog is going to be what s/he gets when s/he does something, right? The class dispersed that night, to meet again the following week.

Surprisingly, Zoë passed puppy class. I thought about enrolling her in Level II but then decided against it. She was better behaved, and she was learning to listen to me. It is important that a dog learns to pay attention to you and no one else but you.

We decided to venture out into the world. She needed exercise; I needed exercise, so what would become a nightly ritual began shortly after. Every night, as the sun was falling in the sky, we would walk around our neighborhood. I was renting a studio apartment at that time in my life, as that was all I could afford. We ventured out, gradually expanding the perimeter of our walks. We got up to about two miles a night.

As I have written about before, I was still struggling with my shyness...believing the world was a dangerous place to live. We did find safe places to walk as we ventured out.

We would have people approach us, including adults, adults with babies in strollers, and adults with small children. It never ceased to amaze me that even children knew she was a poodle. Perhaps because of the way she was cut (not frou-frou, but in a simple short puppy-cut), but they still knew. The kids would yell at her from across the street... "Oh, look at the giant poodle!" I would laugh and smile. Some parents would let their children ask me to pet her. They were fascinated by her fluffy hair, particularly on the top of her hair (otherwise known as her topknot). She didn't like being approached that way, kids reaching for the top of her head, but rather from below, to have her chin scratched.

I learned to teach the kids how to interact with her, as well as the parents...along with lessons such as: one should never tease a dog, run from a dog, or any other inappropriate gestures with a dog. Somehow, I learned to interact with everyone who approached us. Sometimes it was a "no thank you, we're just going to keep on walking," to a full halt to let the children and the giant poodle interact.

I learned that people's motives in the world weren't always malicious. I started to believe that sometimes people were just looking for some type of love and affection, and to interact with the giant poodle. Believe it or not, I slowly began seeing humans for their humanity, and their genuineness when all they wanted to do was pet my dog. This softened me; this made me less afraid of people.

That was Zoë's gift to me...to get me back in touch with the world, to not be afraid of the world or the people in it. People are generally good-natured and willing to treat others like they would want to be treated. I was brought out of my shell, out of darkness, and into the light of day to see people, to know people, and to interact with their good intentions. People aren't so scary. They are just like you and me...only they wanted to pet "the giant poodle with the fluffy hair!"

This was my life lesson. Her gift to me. This is what began my life-long journey of breaking out of my shell and realizing that people aren't so scary after all. Thank you, Zoë. From the bottom of my heart, thank you. May you rest in peace with Stella, Safina, and Macy. Please look after each other. I miss you every day.

One-Liner: Having Zoë began my journey to being a "recovered" shy person. Generally speaking, the world is a safe place...we just have to go out and experience it and welcome the kindness of strangers. It's okay to be open to interacting with others. More than not, they are genuine, kind, and love dogs. I remember this time in my life as being full of personal growth. And remember, I believe our life lessons can come from anywhere...even our dogs...if we just stay open to receiving them.

{ 47 }

A Sample...

...in my spare time, when I am not watching the Buckeyes, with my husband or my dog, I like to write films. I started my master's in fine arts (MFA) degree, in Screenwriting. And, since this is a book about healing myself, I thought I would put in a sample of a screenplay. It is one thing to have a fictional story in your head, but quite another to write it as a script.

There are formatting rules that are so specific, to go from "I have a great idea for a movie," to something that can actually be put on a screen as a watchable, heart-capturing visual story, is quite another.

For example, each line for a scene must contain the following for the director to follow: First, you must specify if the scene is taking place inside (INT) or outside (EXT); second, where the scene is taking place, at a particular local (e.g., University Sports Arena); finally, you must decide what time of day it is, (9AM or DAYTIME, NIGHTIME). This line in a script is called a "slugline." Altogether, it looks something like:

INT. SIDELINE BASKETBALL SPORTS ARENA – 9PM – NIGHT

I go into detail about this, because writing a screenplay is a very complex process. A stage play, for example, has a very different structure to it, having to identify "props" for property used on stage; "noises" for any noise the audience might hear – all very specific and all very detailed.

Once an author has the formatting issue down, I find it a lot of fun to present your ideas visually in a way that someone reading the script knows exactly who is where at all times, in all moments. Just as the director must know these things, so should the writer and the reader. As this is how actors decide what films to star in and the casting agent who to cast. As a screenwriter, I have won awards for my screenplay, SUPPOSED TO BE.

I can write my pain into characters in a movie. I can let my anger come through as part of, say, an interrogation scene in a film. If you understand the structure of a script or stage play, and put your ideas into that structure, half of the process is over. It is very cathartic to let characters experience your pain rather than you, yourself. To me, this is an extremely rewarding process. cathartic even. But then the real challenge begins: finding someone else to see your vision the way you do. This is where I have dropped out of the process…as I have found it difficult to find producers or even an agent to market your film. SUPPOSED TO BE won many awards, got the attention of a couple of producers, but I didn't have any money to put towards the production or know the right people.

There are even what're called "loglines." These are usually one to two sentences giving the plot of the story. For example, SUPPOSED TO BE's logline goes something like, "After a young woman takes her life by suicide, she must work on all of her issues that got her to that point with the help of an unlikely healer."

For the script I am currently working on, the logline reads something like, "An abused black girl becomes a successful African American attorney and must confront her past after killing an innocent woman in a post-traumatic flashback."

I have always dreamed of "writing movies." So much so that, as a child, I said that I would write movies that would star Tom Cruise and Denzel Washington. That was my written down dream as a teenager. I peaked late in life...a late bloomer...no reason this cannot still happen...right?

In the meantime, I wrote a "snippet" of a script so that the readers can see what a movie looks like on paper (see below). First, a comment on the process.

Dialogue. As a psychologist, I feel pretty strongly about the words I choose; they are in a particular order, punctuation, emphasis on words, etc. It is all presented to the reader in a very purposeful way. Everything; ...all of it.

I thought I would include a small example from the mind of a screenwriter, someone who has an idea for a story and what is necessary for it to be put on the "big screen," as it known post-COVID, when everything seems to go immediately to a streaming device and a small screen, instead of the typical movie-sized screen.

Be they stories with characters, poems, journaling, any type of writing can release what is inside you. And I will say, at this point in my life, unmatched was the moment I heard my words acted and spoken on a stage. There is no other feeling like it. And to have people laugh at the times you intended, when you wrote the script; and similarly, cry. It is the best feeling in the world.

So, here I will share a short scene that I created so that everyone can understand the format of a screenplay, the delicacy that I put in every word, and how it affects you, the reader.

<u>SIDELINE</u>

FADE IN

INT. CROWDED COLLEGE BASKETBALL SPORTS ARENA – NIGHT

First-time sideline reporter, JESSICA, African American, 30's, dressed in on-camera live reporting "sports-wear," is on the sidelines of a basketball arena. It is halftime and the atmosphere is electric. Players, cheerleaders, staff, band members, students all whizzing by her. Her eyes are wide. CAMERAMAN, Caucasian, 40's, in behind-the-camera, slouch-wear, is in front of her, behind the camera adjusting lens.

JESSICA
How do I look?

CAMERAMAN
(mono-toned, almost sarcastic)
Gorgeous.

He turns the light on her.

JESSICA
(shielding her eyes)
Oh, my goodness, that's bright.

CAMERAMAN
All right. Here comes the team. The coach will be next.

JESSICA
I'm nervous.

CAMERAMAN
We've been over this a thousand times.
You are ready, sweetie. You're gonna be great.

Jessica primps.

CAMERAMAN (CONT'D)
Here he comes.
(beat)

JESSICA
Coach!

COACH, tall, African American male, wearing dark suit approaches her. He is at least a foot taller than Jessica, forcing him to lean down to answer her questions; and forces her to lean into him to ask her questions.

CAMERAMAN
We're live in 3, 2...
(points to her)

JESSICA
A couple words before the start of the second half?

COACH

Sure.

JESSICA
Your team is down by 7. What are your
thoughts going into the second half?

COACH
Well, Jessica, I'll tell you,
our defense has got to step up. We're not
getting enough boards. We're not executing
our set plays. Both sides really, offensively and
defensively. We gotta tighten up.

Crowds are rushing by them, noise is escalating, band is playing, all causing them to have to lean into one another even further. Jessica's eyes widen, a bit star-struck.

JESSICA
Tighten up?

She reaches out and straightens his tie.

COACH
We just look sloppy. Unorganized.

She brushes some lint off his suit jacket.

JESSICA
And your 3-point shooters?

She flips her hair.

COACH

Yeah, we gotta give them opportunities. But first, get some penetration in the
paint first.

She adjusts his pocket square.

> JESSICA
> Yeah, you do.

> COACH
> Once we do that, we'll find our outside shooters. It's all about rhythm.

> JESSICA
> Yeah, it is.
> (beat)
> You know, Coach. I gotta say, you really wear that suit.

Sexual tension between them is rising – she is flirting, he is sweating, awkwardness mounting. The words become very sexualized.

> COACH
> (embarrassed)
> Well, thank...

> JESSICA
> And the pink tie and pocket square?
> Is that for Breast Cancer Awareness Month?

> COACH
> Yes, ma'am.

> JESSICA

Save the ta-ta's! Am I right?

Cameraman is signaling her to wrap it up.

> JESSICA (CONT'D)
> Y'all have a good second half now, sugar!

> COACH
> Ma'am?

> JESSICA
> I don't wanna have this same conversation at the end of the game!
> (laughing nervously)
> You know what I'm sayin'?

> COACH
> (sweat beading on his forehead)
> No, I'm not really sure. What's happening here.

> JESSICA
> Go on now. Go get 'em, Coach.
> (awkward BEAT)
> I'll see YOU after the game!

Coach awkwardly backs away from Jessica to disengage, holding his hand up to be cordial.

> JESSICA
> You get it tight, now! You FIND that rhythm!
> Go on now!

Jessica pats the coach on his behind as he walks away. She is still talking into the microphone and camera is still rolling.

JESSICA (CONT'D)
It's good from behind too!
Yeah, it is!
(guttural)
Umm!

JESSICA (CONT'D)
(yelling after him)
And don't you go losin' that suit, now!
Ya hear?! Or the game neither!

Coach begins jogging toward the locker room. Playfully, he lifts up his suit jacket from behind and does a little dance with his ass.

JESSICA (CONT'D)
(watching after him)
(guttural, loud)
Umm-umm, UMM! Now, that's what I'm talkin' about!

Jessica turns back around to face the camera. She is fanning herself with the notecards in her hand.

JESSICA (CONT'D)
This is Jessica Simpson, no – not that Jessica
Simpson – girlfriend's black, oh-kay! - and
I'll see you after the game. And Coach Hayes!
(beat)
Chip, Ryan, back to you in the studio.

Cameraman hangs his head in defeat. Camera is still rolling.

POV through camera lens. Jessica approaches camera, her hair mussed, her lipstick smeared a bit, wide-eyed but for a different reason.

>JESSICA (CONT'D)
>Did you get it? All of it...you got it, right?

>CAMERAMAN
>(head hanging, shaking his head)
>Yeah...I got it.

Jessica is still fanning herself. She strikes a pose: other hand in the air, tosses her hair, licks her lips, hand on hip, panting. She's a sweaty mess but so proud of her first on-air appearance. Cameraman is still shaking his head behind the camera.

>JESSICA
>Nailed him!

A look of surprise comes over her face. She's bent over at the waist, panting, hands on her knees. She does the ceremonial "mic-drop." She scrambles to pick up the mic and put it back to her mouth.

>JESSICA (CONT'D)
>I mean "it!"
>(beat)
>Nailed it!

>CAMERAMAN
>Jesus, Jessica! We're still live...

Jessica stood there awkwardly still, a smile plastered realized she was still being delivered "live" to the city's own local broadcast.

BOTH/JESSICA & CAMERAMAN
SHIT!

FADE OUT

One-Liner: This is not about the actual script as much as it is about sharing a part of me with you. This is what I believe: cultivating that side that we all have makes us unique. Whatever that is for you, celebrate it, share it, don't share it, but please, embrace it for yourself. My play, DO YOU SEE ME?, had a 2-week sold-out run. It's review: good, but dark. It was a dark time in my life. I put it into a story and put it on a stage for everyone to watch. Vulnerable? Absolutely. Hearing my words spoken on a stage: exhilarating.

{ 48 }

Bob's Barricades...

...as with any bustling metropolitan area, there is always construction going on. Whether it is a building going up or repaving the roads, it is always in progress, and it is always an inconvenience for those who are trying to get where we need to go.

Recently, I was driving home from work and saw more orange barrels. I looked at one of them while I was at a stoplight long enough to notice that all of the barrels and blockades had the words BOB'S BARRICADES on them in black paint. So, naturally, I started thinking about Bob. First, I wondered if he had some kind of "corner" on the barricade market just in my town or if his barricades were in other towns as well. Then I wondered if this was Bob's only job, or if maybe it was just a side gig all the while, or if he was really doing something else all day.

I wondered what Bob's life might be like—*did he have a wife or a partner...children...a dog, did he make a decent living?* Then, as human beings do (or at least, this one), I started thinking about my life as compared to Bob's. I bet Bob doesn't have to hear about a wife wanting to kill her husband and the traumatized man coming to him for help. I bet Bob doesn't have to cope with other people's daily depression and anxiety, have conversations about drugs and alcohol, psychiatric medication, divorce, parenting, and working for an unreasonable boss. I bet Bob doesn't have to worry that his clients might kill themselves or someone else—and if they do, would *he* blame himself, or at least not be legally liable?

Man, Bob must have it easy. All he has to do is make sure the right number of barricades get delivered to the right place at the right time. Although, he probably has people to do that for him. Yeah, he's probably outsourced that responsibility. At worst, maybe Bob has to worry about corralling his barricades if one gets loose or somehow wanders away from the herd. Or maybe, worse yet, maybe one gets run over by a car or gets tagged by graffiti, but apparently, the supply of Bob's barricades is endless, as I see them all over town, no matter the location, the construction, or the project. It seems Bob has cornered the barricade market, at least in this town. And I imagine Bob's life to be easy, comparatively speaking. But, then again, I don't know Bob; I don't know anything about his life, his struggles, his trials, or tribulations. Maybe I hope Bob has an easier emotional life than mine. That's what I hope for Bob. And, yes, this entire conversation took place in my head while waiting my turn at a stoplight.

One-Liner: Everyone has a story...a job like Bob's seems like it would be easier than the one I have; there are so many variables; how could I possibly know Bob has a job that is easier than mine? Bob may have more different struggles than I have. Maybe I don't want Bob's job. I would like to spend an evening sitting around Bob's kitchen table and hear what he and his family talk about. We are all just trying to make our way in the world. Whatever your way is, be the best at it, corner the market on it, embrace it – be it – love it...or at least like it.

{ 49 }

Music...

...recently, I've been concerned that I have not been listening to music. I don't listen to any of my devices with songs I have downloaded. I don't listen to music in my car. I get irritated when my husband plays music in the house. I don't want to hear it.

Music has always played an important part in my life. Like anyone else, it can bring me up when I'm down; it can "rally" me when I'm about to do something important; it can bring me to tears when I'm already down. It can make me dance. It can calm me down. The most concerning of all is that I usually listen to music when I write. But lately, nope, nuh-uh, nada, not interested. And I have no idea why.

Now, it is true that in the last couple of years, my husband has become part of a rock band, covering songs from the 1960s and 1970s through the present. I was the one who pushed him to get back into drumming (he was a drummer all through college), as he had given up music since his dedication to architecture. I have been involved as a little more than a fan but a little less than a "groupie" or a roadie.

I have provided endless moral support for him and the others in the band—which I might argue is more exhausting than "just following" the band around. So, maybe I am getting my music "fix" from that and don't feel the need to keep it incorporated into my daily life. I must admit, it does concern me. I can remember all the way back to my undergraduate years and doing my statistics homework while listening to U2's album *Rattle and Hum* on my portable CD player through my earphones to drown out the noise from sharing a dorm suite with three other women. But, as I say, in life, while writing, and in therapy—trust the process. I trust that when my brain is ready to re-incorporate music into my life, other than that of my husband's band, I will let it happen organically. Maybe it won't happen at all. Sitting through a three-hour gig, three to four hours of my life, may be all the music I need right now. I delight in watching him play, delight in watching him enjoy what he is doing, and delight in learning the words to all of the band's songs. Maybe that is sufficient. Either way, I will let that be enough and trust that music doesn't need to be in my life right now...any more than it already is.

One-Liner: I admit music affects me emotionally...sometimes too much...I think music in my life has a place and a time...it may not be now for a reason. Perhaps my life doesn't have a place or time in it right now. Perhaps I've become just more noise-sensitive in my older age. Or maybe I'm just not down with what the kids are listening to these days. Regardless, music, like any phase, will just come and go as it pleases. That, I believe in—phases.

{ 50 }

Motherfucking Quality Time...

...so, by now, I am fairly certain most people are familiar with *The Five Love Languages* by Gary Chapman. It happened to make a resurgence in my life around the time I married my husband.

A colleague and I were gathering materials to take to a New Employee Orientation Fair and were looking for an activity that the employees could get some credit for when they stopped by our booth. I had the crazy idea to print a free Love Languages quiz off the internet and take it as our activity. It was a shortened quiz, and I'm not even sure it was written or copyrighted by Dr. Chapman. Nonetheless, I thought it seemed like a good idea and interesting enough to get new employees' attention to bring them to our booth, which was why we were really there—for them to learn about the Employee Assistance Program at the University of Florida. I think it was successful.

What I had not anticipated was taking two copies of the quiz home with me that night and taking it with my now-husband. We laid down to take it together. The results of that quiz changed our relationship, or should I say, it changed me *in* our relationship. Turns out my husband's love language is "quality time." That's right, motherfucking "quality time."

Why my hostility towards that stupid quiz? Suddenly, after ten years with this man, the quiz was telling me, "You have to give up some of your cherished time by yourself, you silly introvert, and give it to your husband because that is his love language." All those trips to the grocery store to get you your favorite foods, flowers, and favorite drinks from Starbucks...I was now faced with the idea of having to be in the car with him while he was doing all of those things for me. I no longer got to lounge and have the house to myself and get the things I love because I was in this relationship with a man to whom it was more important that I be with him than anything else I could do for him: to have me in the car with him while he was getting those things for me (my love language); *that's* what is most important to the most important man in my life. And there went my entire plan to selfishly recharge in solitude. To this day, his favorite thing to do is take Sunday drives in the pouring rain, with our dog on my lap, and spend motherfucking quality time in the car talking while we drive around. For the love of God!

One-Liner: Ain't that some shit; after ten years, you think you know someone, and out of nowhere, I have to spend motherfucking quality time with a man, my man, so he doesn't go on out and find his quality time with someone else if you know what I mean!

{ 51 }

The House, the Kids...

...and The Ohio State Football Tickets...

...so, my parents got divorced in 1981 or 1982, I'm not sure. It wasn't a great time in our life as a family. Regardless of getting into who did what to whom between my mom and dad, there is a funny story that came out of it.

When the court date came for my parents' divorce, I didn't even think my father was there. But my mom was. And she was fully prepared to get what she wanted. My understanding was she had an excellent attorney, one of the best in Columbus. She says that the way the divorce hearing went was something like the judge looked at her over his half-glasses, and he asked her what she wanted out of the divorce, so the story goes. She looked back at him, not really getting into why she didn't want the divorce in the first place, and responded, "I want the house, the kids, and The Ohio State football tickets." And that's exactly what she got. She got my brother and me, the house they had built together in about 1966, which she continued to live in until about 2018 or 2019, and season tickets to every home game (and some away) the Ohio State Buckeye football team played until the day my father passed away. I think this is why sports fanaticism runs on my mother's side, as my dad could not have cared less about the tickets until the day he died.

Every year, we would go through this heinous process of the ticket application going to my dad. My brother or I would intercept it, bring it to my mom, which she would fill out, and give it back to my dad, which he would submit, paying for it on a credit card, and my mom would write him a check. Turns out, the tickets came to be worth thousands of dollars, just face value. They were worth much more as the team went on to win national championships and is still a contender at the end of most football seasons, even now, and are coached by some of the finest: Jim Tressel and Urban Meyer and Ryan Day.

I've been lucky enough to watch Urban Meyer take the University of Florida Gators to a national title and the Ohio State Buckeyes. Thousands of dollars my mom would make on a rainy Michigan day from those tickets, through which she would decide to stay home and watch it on TV with a fire and a Bloody Mary. As anyone who is a good Buckeye knows, the Michigan game is played on the Saturday after Thanksgiving and starts at high noon, so morning adult beverages are the order of the day. And that, my friends, is how you get season tickets to one of the most winningest college football franchises in the country.

The happy ending to this story isn't about the tickets, but it is that as devastated as my mom was during the divorce, she happily married my stepfather in 1984, and they just celebrated their fortieth anniversary with a family reunion cruise, paid for by my stepfather for ten of us.

One-Liner: Know what you want, ask for what you want, get what you want, and receive the benefits of what you want.

{ 52 }

The Last Autograph...

...genuinely, I feel it is important for you to know that I couldn't make these stories up if I tried. The year was 2007, and Tim Tebow of the University of Florida won the Heisman Trophy. He happened to have a route on his scooter he would take first thing in the morning, past my office building while I was walking to my office at the University of Florida at the same time. On the Monday after winning the Heisman, "Timmy," as he was known around campus, was scootin' by me, and out of nowhere, I yelled out, "Hey, Timmy!" like we were friends. Sure enough, he was a nice enough young man that he put the brakes on his scooter and stopped.

I ran over to the median where he was stopped, now in front of my office building; I introduced myself and asked him if I could have an autograph. I am quite certain that he does not remember this, except that he remembers the time when some crazy lady stopped him for an autograph. I told him I was a psychologist in the Student Health Care Center just across the street as I scrambled through my bag, which apparently contained everything but a blank sheet of paper in it. As I continued to look for paper and a pen, a crowd started to gather. I was talking nonsensically to him, telling him that I was from Columbus, Ohio, and I was a Buckeye, but, you know, "Go Gators" when in Rome, as they say. About five minutes and fifty people later, I handed him a piece of paper and said, "Please make it out to Dr. Blue." And he did.

I am now the proud owner of an authentic autograph from Tim Tebow, quarterback of the University of Florida Gators and 2007 Heisman Trophy winner, that reads: To Dr. Blue – Go Gators! God Bless, Timmy Tebow #15.

The very next day, there was a public announcement to the entire University of Florida (60,000+ students strong) that Mr. Tim Tebow was *no longer* allowed to be stopped and asked to sign autographs. I like to think I got the (or one of the) last autographs he gave at the University of Florida.

One-Liner: He is as God-fearing, attractive, and genuine in person as he appears on TV; if you are going to chase down a famous sports figure for an autograph, for the love of God, please have a paper and pen on hand, for the second time.

{ 53 }

The "Bystander Effect," NOT...

...this incident happened a bit more recently. My husband and I took in his elderly parents about one and a half years ago. The four of us now live in a lovely house near the Research Triangle in North Carolina. Besides being an architect, it is noteworthy that my father-in-law is a retired professor of architecture at the University of Florida and also a writer. My mother-in-law is a semi-retired weaver and fully retired blood bank worker at the University of Florida. Their professions have less to do with my story than the fact that my husband and I had lived with them before, outside of Gainesville, Florida, while I was going through a couple of bad patches in my life. I have no children; they have accepted me into their family since I met their son, so it is my turn to give back to those who have helped me.

As I said, recently, I was at a day-long conference put on by the university's police department on the "de-escalation of irate students or patients." A retired local chief of police gave the presentation, which was outstanding, as he was quite a character with lots of colorful stories to tell. As you may know by now, my husband is also a drummer. He had taken me to the workshop held at a hotel on campus that day. He happened to have a gig that night, which started at five p.m. We were booked to be at the workshop until five p.m. but were guaranteed to be done by four p.m. I texted my husband, who was leaving at three p.m. for his gig, to have his ninety-year-old parents pick me up on campus.

At about 4:15 p.m., he closed the presentation, but I had to go to use the restroom. As I was leaving the bathroom, I saw my dog on a leash outside the conference room doors, which meant his parents had arrived to fetch me. I quickened my step, knowing that if I got outside and my dog saw me before my father-in-law, who was holding her leash, did, she was going to try to run to me and pull my father-in-law down, and it would be a whole thing in front of about fifty police officers. So, I stayed quiet and out of her sightline as I approached them. Once near their car, I said my dog's name, and she oriented toward me; she turned and lunged in my direction, as I suspected she would. I, in turn, lunged toward her and my father-in-law as to lessen the space between us so he wouldn't get pulled down. In doing so, I neglected to look down and saw that I was stepping onto a wheelchair ramp built into the corner of the parking lot. Well, down I went! Wearing a lovely blue dress and pink blazer, it was me who ended up face down in the parking lot. (Even disabled folk miss a step or two while trying to get to other disabled folks.)

As soon as I was on the ground, three male police officers came to my aid to pick me up. I was mortified. As soon as they gathered me and my things, I hopped up quickly, pretending to be fine. After thanking them profusely, I proceeded to get the dog in the backseat of the car and jumped in myself; my tail tucked firmly under my behind. My mother-in-law was laughing, as was my father-in-law. (I'm sure it was funny from where they were sitting/standing.) I was in a state of embarrassed shock!

And just after having gone over the Bystander Effect, a term used by social psychologists to describe the apathy that comes with watching something bad happen to other people and *not* stepping in to help because we believe someone else will intervene. Well, I tell you what, those three armed men were by my side as soon as I hit the pavement. There was no Bystander Effect going on in that parking lot that day. I sure hope neither of the chiefs of police who were there saw nor the two women from my office who were there as well. Mortified!

My husband's first question upon hearing this story was, "Did your dress flip up over your head?" He thought maybe I had flashed the entire police force, which I might have, now that I think about it. I had scrapes on both my knees but no holes in my dress. Oh, Lord.

We went home, I licked my wounds, literally and metaphorically, got changed and I drove my parents-in-law to my husband's gig a half-hour away. Without him knowing the whole story, I stared at him up on stage that night, wondering if he knew how lucky he was to have married me! I'm not sure why I went there with my story in my head, but I did, still shaken by what had happened.

One-Liner: Let's hope as a society that the Bystander Effect will become a thing of the past and people will be more helpful and kind to one another and intervene if another person is in trouble, as I appeared to be.

{ 54 }

A Final (i.e., Lasting) Word...

...so, I was in my favorite consignment shop, browsing as they were "assessing" my donations, which can take hours, and I'm fairly certain is a racket, but I browsed as I waited. I came across a small wood-framed canvas with an interesting quote on it. Also written was Dr. Seuss's name. I'm not sure who coined it, as I have seen iterations of it before. The quote was about being active in this moment, to reflect how you want to be remembered tomorrow.

I return to the issues of one's own mortality. For some un-Godly reason, words about being present today and not worrying about the past or the future take me straight to thinking about my own mortality. I don't know why... I end up there in the most circuitous ways, this being one of them. Questions like: who am I...how did I get here...where am I going...and what will happen to me along the way? Immediately come into my mind. It used to scare me. Now, it inspires me, motivates me, and challenges me. If there is no inherent meaning, it is up to me to create meaning out of a finite, inherently meaningless state. Be better; choose better; live better; hold on to the good and bad because both will happen to you. Be the best-est version of yourself always and forever. You are only responsible to the person who looks back at you in the mirror. As long as you are proud of who you see, you're gonna be fine. If not, right the wrongs...do what it takes to be the person you would want as a friend. Fix it. Be it. Forgive it, whether it is something you do or something done to you. Accept it…and keep it moving. It is life; it is your life, and only you can make it what you want or need. Only you can do that. If the Universe is never wrong, then there is meaning in all we do. I'm merely suggesting that you own it, take responsibility for it, and treasure it—even the bad—for that makes you the human being you are today.

One-Liner: Be present…be good…forgive yourself…and accept who you are and what you stand for today. Tomorrow is promised to no one. Be who you are, accept who you are, change who you are, but, most of all…love who you are.

{ 55 }

Sadness, Lobsters, and Existentialism...

...I woke up today ready to write. I have two good stories I was going to use in this book. But suddenly, I am filled with sadness. Overcome, really. I don't know where it comes from. I can't figure it out. I won't spend much time on it because I know it's not coming from anywhere in particular. I didn't look in the mirror (that makes me sad). Nobody has died. I might have had a bad dream. That makes me sad sometimes. It's raining. That also makes me sad sometimes. I'm not really getting along with my husband. That kind of makes me sad, not really, though. My tailbone hurts—like a bed sore almost—because I haven't gotten out of bed yet and it is four p.m. That makes me sad.

I made the mistake of watching TikTok and looking at Facebook. That didn't really make me sad. All I watch on there are funny animal videos. I got a picture today texted to me of live lobsters in the Northeast with their pinchers closed with rubber bands, all in a tank in a restaurant waiting to be chosen to be cooked and eaten. They were moving around the tank, restricted, out of their natural habitat. That made me sad. I'm not a vegetarian or someone who does not eat living things. My dog is with me. She licks my tears. Probably because they're salty, but I pretend it is because she doesn't want me to be sad...she doesn't want me to be sad.

So, I'm left with the inevitable. Sadness is sadness. It's like cancer is cancer. It doesn't discriminate. I mean, you must be kind to your body, e.g., not smoke or drink to excess, to not provoke cancer. But some people get it for absolutely no reason. Maybe genetics, I guess. But the point is, I'm sad today because I'm sad. It is mental illness. It is depression. No matter how much I don't want it, it doesn't matter. I didn't do anything wrong. I'm not being punished. I know it will stop. I don't really know when. I don't drink. I don't use illicit drugs. I don't feel that I am doing anything wrong to warrant this affliction.

Let me take a minute to reflect on sadness. It is so isolating. It makes me feel so misunderstood. Of course, there are things I'm grateful for (gratitude exercise); of course, I can name three good things in my life right now (Three Good Things exercise). There are people in my life who say they love me. There are people I love in my life. Right? There is no logical reason for me to be sad. It is an illness. It takes over me. It will consume me. I will ride it out, like anything else. It feels like the tears won't stop. I know they will. I'm not thinking about anything sad except maybe the lobsters. I wouldn't want anyone to restrain me. I wouldn't want to know that I am going to die. I don't think lobsters have brains. I don't think they have feelings. At least, I hope not.

So, maybe their lives are coming to an inevitable end, and they don't know or care. It doesn't seem right that they are restrained in a tank, but I might be, quite possibly, the only person who cares about the lobsters. I know they are not mammals. They are invertebrates with localized collections of neuronal cell bodies called ganglia, according to Siri, so, not exactly the brains you and I have. In other words, they don't do a lot of thinking, other than doing what is necessary to survive. So, their lives might end soon, those in the tank, but they're not having an existential crisis about it. They aren't sad.

PEARLS AND PURSE STRAPS... OR HOW A SHRINK "SHRINKS" HERSELF

My husband just came in and said goodbye, as he has a gig tonight. His only words to me were, "What's wrong? Really? You're crying? I have to go. See you." He's used to it. What he is saying is, "I don't have time for this," which is true, and maybe "I don't really care," as this is also usually true. He has to get to his gig, and he thinks I only get upset when he leaves me, like for a show or to travel out of state. That is not actually the case. I guess it was when we first moved here, and he would have to travel out of the state. But, again, not really. It doesn't bother me anymore. Alas, he may overestimate his importance in my life, but I'll give him that one, meaning I think we all think that. Sometimes, he forgets that I lived forty-nine years without him. Anyway, the only ones who will really understand this chapter are those who have experienced genuine depression. Sadness for no reason. It sucks. I don't even think it's cathartic at this point. I must just wait for it to pass.

People get mad at you for being sad. It's true. Especially family, I have found. Doctors don't understand it. Friends don't understand it. Family members definitely don't understand it. Rather than share, here I sit (lie), crying all by myself. It hurts my head. It hurts my brain. It hurts my soul. It hurts my being. The good news is that I am used to it, and it will pass. I don't have any physical pain to speak of. Sometimes, when this happens, I wish I did. (Well, "wish" is a strong word.) Physical pain distracts me from my mental pain. There are even times when I feel like I may actually lose my mind, and suddenly, I am struck down with a physical ailment. All to distract me from what is going on for me emotionally, I believe. It happens at the oddest times, but when it does happen, I know why, and no matter what physical pain, at least it distracts me from my psychological pain. I don't know when. I took my medicine. Maybe an hour or so ago. I'll live. Like any other kind of acute illness, I just have to wait it out. I will. Maybe I'll play a game on my computer to distract myself. I'll stop thinking about the lobsters that I can control.

One-Liner: Sadness sometimes comes without reason; don't fight it; don't let others tell you it's ridiculous; take your medication; distract yourself; and, whatever you do, don't think about the lobsters, that is sad...poor lobsters.

{ 56 }

It Is a Lovely Day…

…Until Somebody Hits the Pavement…

…I suppose this is somewhat akin to the old saying, "It's all fun and games until someone loses an eye." And that comparison is not wrong. It was July 4th, and my husband got us tickets right behind the Durham Bulls' dugout, maybe three rows back, for their game that evening. Perfect seats, perfect weather (except it was a little hot and humid—which you would think I'm used to, having lived in Godforsaken northern central Florida for almost twenty years), perfect hot dogs, perfect pretzels, perfect sodas (for me) and beers (for the rest of the family). Even perfect selfies! How often does that happen? (Well, not so often for me, as I'm not part of the "that is not your angle" generation). It really was perfect.

We had made it to our seats okay. My husband had dropped us off in front of the stadium and went to park the car. He met us at our seats. We were settled into our seating chart (girl, boy, girl, boy). Oh, and it was the Fourth of July.

As an aside, I hate the Fourth of July—as I come from a place that takes it so seriously that I've dreaded it since high school. We would gather at friends' houses. I would always feel bad about how I was dressed (See Chapter 22). I was not drinking, but everyone else was. I was hot, hair frizzed from the humidity, everybody else drinking, often raining, mosquitos out in the thousands, I'm pretty sure...ugh...you get the idea. The Fourth of July! So, as "4th's" go, this was truly a perfect day. Even the baseball game was great.

It was the bottom of the ninth, the Bulls last at-bat, down 5-0, and hit after hit kept coming out of the dugout. Everyone around us was going crazy. It really all happened so fast. Bases were loaded multiple times. And one by one, the RBIs just kept coming in. Full count, bases loaded, two strikes, and holy moly, the winning scorer was waved home from the third base coach, and the game ended with the Bulls winning 6-5! It was crazy! The perfect game for the perfect day!

All in the timing...

The sun was setting. All that was left was the highly anticipated fireworks display. First, we all stood and sang the National Anthem again, as it was the Nation's birthday, after all. There were military people out on the field, the flag waving in the barely noticeable breeze, and the big wagon had been pulled out to center field from which the fireworks would ignite. No one left, not an empty seat. After the National Anthem, there was a countdown from three, and the stadium went dark. The fireworks went off without a hitch. They were loud, colorful, and synced to music—I remember hearing Katy Perry's "Fireworks" trying to rise above the noise of the crowd. From start to finish, they lasted for fifteen minutes easily, the fireworks. It was a day and night I will never forget, even if the story ended there. But, alas, it didn't.

We had our last chat, the four of us, before my husband left to go get the car, which he would then pick us up right in front of the stadium, where he had dropped us off. We have a handicapped placard, as my husband's parents are ninety, and the EMT would later tell my husband that was the "best description of someone's medical history he had ever heard."

My father-in-law, mother-in-law, and I sat in our seats for probably a half-hour before we decided to make our way to the entrance. This would give my husband a chance to get the car from the garage where he had parked and make his way to the entrance. The three of us finally make it to the entrance. I figure my husband is coming any minute. I decided to run into the gift shop to buy a couple of golfing shirts for my brother, as his birthday was July 1. (These shirts would later be used as a pillow. Who knew?)

I was standing out by the curb so I could wave to my husband as soon as I saw the car, and the parking attendants could let him through the cones to retrieve us. I must have been standing there for an hour. I was sweating, with zero tolerance for the heat; my in-laws were trying to make the best of waiting by leaning against the gradated stones leading up to the fountain. I was so focused on not missing my husband that I did not see my mother-in-law hit the pavement.

I heard my father-in-law calling my name from behind me, trying to tell me something was wrong with his wife, Jan. I hurried over; she had passed out and was lying on the pavement in front of the entrance to the ballpark. She was barely conscious, and by then, a park EMS was tending to her. Her blood pressure was sky-high, her heart was beating quickly, and she started to vomit. Just about then, my husband finally arrived. I was drenched with sweat. He was so irritated about not being able to get out of the parking garage sooner. My father-in-law, Ron, was overwhelmed by the EMS woman yelling at Jan to ask her questions because we were still next to the fountain, and no one could hear each other. He wanted something to use as a pillow to put under her head, so I gave him the bag with the golf shirts I had just bought. It was then decided that an ambulance needed to be called. Having enough medical knowledge to know what was going on, I was trying to calm down my husband, whose language was increasingly abusive toward everyone involved, which was not good for anyone.

Ron was overwhelmed by what was happening. My husband was yelling at anyone who would listen. The situation brought out absolutely unexpected behavior from all of them. No, I'm not going to include myself in that, as I was doing what I was told by the emergency medical staff, trying to do what my husband was yelling at me to do and accommodating Ron's request as well. In the minutes between Jan going from the ground to the gurney to the ambulance, the day went from being one of the most beautiful days celebrating our nation's birthday to a trip to the hospital via ambulance with Jan having what they diagnosed with heatstroke. She is okay now.

One-Liner: Be present and enjoy every second of every minute, especially when they seem perfect, because you do not know, let me write that again, you do not know at which second the day may turn on you, and you find yourself following an ambulance, carrying two people you love, to the emergency room.

What we also learn from events like this:
1) Stay hydrated with water when it is hot outside.
2) When someone is fainting, falling, or otherwise headed to a hard surface, do what you can to
prevent a head injury.
3) If you are not feeling well, let those around you know immediately.
4) You will see the most unpredictable behavior out of those you love the most during crises like this.

5) This will likely necessitate a "come to Jesus" meeting about how we act during crises like this one.

{ 57 }

Unnecessary Jostling…

…so, I had my million-dollar idea for an app about ten years ago. It would allow you to store all of the "cards" people used to carry around on their key chains, like for their local pharmacy or grocery store, to get in-store discounts. That one got made before I had even the chance to finish telling someone about my idea. But this time, I think I've got it!

My husband and I were driving to work this morning. Let me back up. About a month ago, I bought a "new" car, meaning new to me, but not new, off the dealership's lot. Sometimes referred to as pre-owned. Suffice it to say, I could never afford a real, brand-new model, so I bought the prettiest used one I could find in the area. For the first time since the car I got when I was sixteen, I feel attached to a vehicle…meaning it is much more part of me than any of the other half-dozen cars I've had in my life. It is so pretty, shiny, and "sexy," as my husband describes it. And it's white! I've never owned a white car before now.

Backing up even further, I should tell you that my husband is a huge fan of what I like to call "The Formula One." For those who might be unaware, this is the sport of racing sleek-looking cars all over the world. I would say it is different than "stock" car races and even a step up from the Indianapolis 500 race that happens annually.

During race season, my husband records every qualifying race up to and including the actual race every week. F1, as is known to most, is to my husband almost what The Ohio State University Buckeyes are to me. Sure, I've watched a little F1, just out of giving supportive motherfuckin' quality time, as discussed previously. And all I can say about that is, I have a huge "celebrity crush" on Lewis Hamilton!

On our way to work this morning, my car made a noise that I had never heard, like a warning bell or "flute-sounding" noise, and a warning light came on near the speedometer. Let me also say at this point that, yes, my car is one of those cars where we discover a new function or trick almost every day. I was a little alarmed, as it was not a sound I had heard, and the light went off before I could see it from the passenger side. I had no idea what it meant.

As usual, I was late for work and asked my husband to get me there in the most expeditious fashion. Mind you, not F1 fashion, but as quickly as possible. As the light and sound were going off, there was a green traffic light ahead of us, and suddenly, my husband was slowing the car down. I said, "Why aren't you going? It's green!"

And he replied, "I don't want any inappropriate jostling of the car," as we had to cross railroad tracks on our way at this particular light.

"What?!"

"You know, the railroad tracks. There is a huge dip in the road just before the tracks, and I wanted to be gentle while going over the tracks and not jostle the car!"

Sure enough, the light turned red while he was on alert from 1) the unknown flute noise we had just heard, 2) my asking for him not to drive the car in F1 fashion, and 3) his respect for the uneven pavement ahead of us that we must traverse before getting to the light. He just stopped the car. The light turned red. So, neither were we jostled nor did we make the light. There we sat, with my dog on my lap, as is the only way she travels in the car when I'm in the passenger seat, with three extra minutes to talk and for me to get a better understanding of why my husband was trying to avoid any "unnecessary jostling" of my pretty, new, shiny, sexy vehicle. And, of course, adding an additional three minutes to my already late arrival time at work.

...back to my app idea! I think cars should be equipped with an "app" or something akin to that, which alerts husbands when they are driving recklessly and not avoiding any unnecessary jostling, as I suspect my husband does as he often drives my car without me in it. That way, I would be alerted, and he would be alerted if and when he put my car through any "unnecessary jostling." It would come with its own noise, designed by me, of course, with its own special little light. You know, the works when it comes to apps. That way, wives and partners everywhere would know if their car was going through any "unnecessary jostling" while they weren't in it! Genius, right?!

One-Liner: Okay...Okay! I'm being driven to work in what I would consider a luxury car by my husband and trying to be a back/front-seat driver, with a poodle on my lap, to protect my new vehicle from his F1 driving and trying to be on time to work. I know...I can't have it all...I am just thankful that someone is willing to put up with my nonsense and get me to work in a safe, timely manner. I do appreciate him and his willingness to even participate in my nonsense. ...I still think it is a cool idea for an app.

{ 58 }

A Work In Progress...

...A Final Comment On the Process...

...doing anything creative is always a "work-in-progress," right? I think, and I could be wrong, that most artists have their own way of knowing if and when something is "done." A symphony, a sculpture, a painting, a poem, a screenplay, a film, a meal—if food is your medium. Is something ever done? And if it is, how do you know when there's little to no room for improvement in something and it is as good as it is going to be? I would say, and I'm a numbers gal, meaning I like percentages and odds, and I will play those odds in life often, that something is finished when it's about ninety percent done. I don't think any artist is ever going to say something is done until it's as good as it's gonna be. Is it ever perfect right out of the gate? Rarely. Especially in such a subjective field like the arts, it is done when the creator says it's done. Sure, editors, critics, and the general populace are all going to have their "opinions" about its own merit or strength, stacked up against its competitors, so to speak.

Here's my problem: I think about the process (when something is becoming what it is going to be) entirely too much. I get stuck sometimes in thinking about the process. Or I just think about it too much. Like writing this book. As I'm editing and developing the content, I'm living in the process.

There's a tradition in the world of psychologists that therapy consists of two parts: the content and the process. This is the easiest and most familiar analogy I can think of to explain what I am saying/writing.

There is "what" you are talking about, which is the "content," and there is the way you are talking about something, which is the "process." There are therapists who focus solely on the content, and there are therapists who solely focus on the process. A good therapist, in my opinion, is able to do both; a great therapist is one who can do both simultaneously while staying present and being in the moment. As a psychologist, I do have a choice, and it is usually what I think is best for the client at any given point in their therapy.

For example, if someone comes to me stating their problem is depression, but they laugh entirely through the first session, nine times out of ten, I will bring that to their attention by saying something like, "I am aware you are here because you are having a problem with depression, but you are laughing as you talk to me about it." I'd usually get something back from them, like, "Yeah, that's my coping mechanism when I'm in a new situation and uncomfortable. I just laugh." I notice the juxtaposition; I name it; he explains it, we deal with the anxiety of coming to your first therapy appointment, and we move on.

My problem, I'm finding, is that I think I'm getting stuck in the "process." As far as my own process of healing, as is the intent, purpose, genre, and meaning of this book, I'm letting my own process of writing it get in the way of its true purpose: healing...and helping...myself and others.

So...what is my advice to someone facing this problem? I wouldn't say don't over-intellectualize. Don't overthink it. Let it be what it wants to be. And be okay with how it gets there. Okay. I get it. I think. Maybe I just wanted to share with you what writing this book has been like for me.

I have felt vulnerable, exposed, raw, good, bad, and everything in between on this journey. It's no wonder that it takes so much strength and bravery to pick up the phone and make a first therapy appointment for yourself. I believe there is a lot of healing that takes place between thinking about making that call, deciding to make the call, making the call, making an appointment, and actually showing up for the appointment. I would say you are probably 75-80 percent "helped" just by doing all of that and actually keeping the appointment. There's a lot of healing going on in just that process alone. That's why I'm not a big fan of same-day appointments. If you are seen as you make the decision to call, I'm not allowing you to start your own healing process.

Whew! That's a lot about the process! I do hope someone benefits from my vulnerability and transparency and makes that first call for themselves.

One-Liner: I'll write it again: I do hope someone benefits from my vulnerability and transparency and, if appropriate, makes that first call for themselves to get help. If it's not helpful, find another therapist. It is sort of like dating and finding a good therapist. Hang in there; the right one is out there. I hope I was the "right" one for people I've been honored to help. Or write it out, like I did. Hopefully, you will see what it takes to "shrink yourself," and you will go the other way and have a real person help you. Until then...keep reading and writing!

Be well and stay safe. ~Dr. Beth-Anne Blue

- The End... -

ABOUT THE AUTHOR

Dr. Beth-Anne Blue is a psychologist, writer, and storyteller with a deep passion for exploring the human experience—both in others and, now, in herself. For over two decades, she has worked as a licensed clinical psychologist across three states, helping individuals navigate the complexities of life, emotion, and identity. With a keen understanding of the mind and heart, she has dedicated her career to guiding people toward healing, clarity, and transformation.

Behind the professional title and years of expertise, Beth-Anne has always been a writer at her core. Her love for words has been quietly simmering beneath the surface, filling journals, drawers, and the margins of her life. Now, she steps into a new role—not just as a psychologist but as the patient, the narrator, and the storyteller of her own truth. Her latest work, *Pearls and Purse Straps*, is a deeply personal collection of reflections and anecdotes that merge her professional insights with the raw honesty of personal experience. Through this book, she invites readers to witness her journey of self-discovery—one that is as introspective as it is universal. With a unique blend of clinical wisdom, warmth, and humor, Dr. Beth-Anne Blue continues to inspire others—not just by listening but by speaking her own truth for the first time. Whether on the page or in the therapy room, she remains committed to the power of storytelling and the endless pursuit of understanding what it truly means to be human.

www.ingramcontent.com/pod-product-compliance
Lightning Source LLC
Chambersburg PA
CBHW070140080526
44586CB00015B/1780